Hidden Surrey
Town & Country

CHRISTOPHER HOWKINS

with illustrations
by the author

GW00726728

COUNTRYSIDE BOOKS
NEWBURY, BERKSHIRE

First Published 1990
© Christopher Howkins 1990

All Rights Reserved.
No reproduction permitted
without the prior permission
of the publisher:

COUNTRYSIDE BOOKS
3 Catherine Road
Newbury, Berkshire

ISBN 1 85306 082 8

Front cover photograph of Esher
taken by Andy Williams

Back cover photograph of the Mosque at Woking
taken by the author

Produced through MRM Associates Ltd., Reading
Typeset by Microset Graphics Ltd., Basingstoke
Printed in England by J. W. Arrowsmith Ltd., Bristol

Contents

Introduction

What the County of Surrey lacks in size it makes up for in variety. There are chalk downs and clay vales, sandhills and heathlands, woods and valleys, all providing more open space per person than many other counties.

Flung all over this pattern is a scattering of towns and villages and they're still very much *country* places.

To explore this pattern is absorbing and most rewarding. For over a hundred years popular guide books have encouraged people to do just that so there hardly seems the need for another guide book. Indeed that was my first reaction on being asked to consider this commission.

I accepted it because the brief was new – to draw attention to subjects that were not the usual guide book material and where that was not possible, to look afresh at familiar subjects and reveal some aspect usually ignored.

Thus this two-volume *Surrey* was undertaken. It has meant visiting every single place in the county and reviewing it afresh and that of course has been very time consuming. Therefore the work has been written in two parts, with the smaller places – hamlets and villages in the countryside – being surveyed first and published already as *Hidden Surrey*.

Now it's the turn of the larger places. You can't divide Surrey places into the convenient categories of 'towns' and 'villages'. Godstone is a village to people driving through but go and explore and you'll find it's two! There's a second part hidden up on the hill. To walk around both takes longer than a town centre like Weybridge. Then there's Cranleigh which I dare not call a small town as it's so proud of its claim to be the largest village in England! What do you call a place like Ashford, once a village and now a large dormitory centre yet with a shopping centre no bigger than Cranleigh's?

No one would argue that Woking is a town but what do you do about its fringe communities like St. John's, Brookwood, Knaphill etc. At times they're fiercely independent; they wouldn't like to be called 'satellites'! One of them, Horsell, was the old medieval village in the heath and so that was placed with the other medieval villages in *Hidden Surrey*. As it joins on to Woking it deserves a place in this volume too. Instead, the medieval village of Old Woking has been included here as it's even more illogical to separate Old Woking from the 'new' one.

Although this is confusing, one thing is very clear:– all places in Surrey have their own distinct character and origins. There are castle towns like Farnham and Reigate, bridge towns like Walton and Leatherhead, royal towns like Guildford and Weybridge, railway towns like Woking and Redhill, the Roman town of Staines, the abbey town of Chertsey and the military town of Camberley. Labels are useless; Farnham is a castle town but is famous as a Georgian town, Guildford is a royal town, a castle town, a river crossing and a market town. Labels are definitely useless; Haslemere can't even find one to fit. It's a commuter town but then so are all the rest. Give up and just enjoy the variety!

You're still likely to ask what sort of place it is and so entries have been given brief overall descriptions. As you will guess from the above comments, it's very easy to find fault with these. They are just to give a flavour of the feast, to help make sense of the present.

Making sense of the present is not easy as the towns rarely have modern comprehensive guide books. Leatherhead is the great exception. The others certainly have books that make good starting points but there's still much to discover and share. The historical development of Surrey's towns is very poorly understood. Attention has been focused on the smaller places and many of these can offer detailed guide books of high quality. The county collection for all places is housed in the Local Studies Department of Guildford Library.

Arrangement of entries

The complexities of our communities are fascinating to unravel but too much for the few pages possible for each place in this book.

There's nothing more infuriating than guides that list points of interest without their locations so here, where possible, they've been strung together in an itinerary which will guide you round and save a lot of energy criss-crossing through the traffic. It means you may miss some things, but on the itinerary you'll find extra pleasures: a smart Regency villa, a colourful front garden, a satisfying view etc.

The Final Selection

First consideration has been given to things that you can go and see and every subject, perhaps recorded years before, was revisited to confirm it still existed. Much had gone. Alarmingly, several of the sections had to be rewritten during the compilation of the book. Redevelopment is the usual cause but fires and runaway lorries have taken their toll too.

While this book is being printed some of its content will be 'redeveloped'. Indeed the side of Staines Market Place, the north side of Staines town centre and the lower side of Reigate are all being proposed, to name but three. It's a mammoth task keeping my information files up to date so I'd appreciate being notified of changes.

As with *Hidden Surrey*, small removable items have been omitted for fear of attracting thieves. Look carefully and you'll find hundreds of little details that please, Victorian cast iron details in particular.

Today's Work

Some of the modern work makes a really worthwhile contribution to the County's architectural heritage. It's worth a considered look – without prejudice. Needless to say, there are buildings which make you long for a large jar of vanishing cream!

Good modern buildings are scattered all over the County. The district with the most is the Borough of Runnymede, particularly around Chertsey and then, slipping over the river into the Borough of Spelthorne, there are good ones around Staines; have a look at the round one now used by British Gas, built initially for Ready-Mix Concrete.

Guildford buildings have generated intense argument for years. Now, at last it's getting work of a higher quality – have a look at the Research Park and the Riverside Business Park.

Having asked for years why multi-storey car parks always look like concrete sandwiches, there's a new one in Woking that does not. It seems to take Eastern inspiration from Oriental Road etc. although the towers inspire jibes about frontier posts. Being different is never easy!

Too much blame is often thrown at the Planning Committees which isn't fair. Envisaging the future look of some plans is very challenging. I've admired architects' drawings in an estate agent's window only to look later at the completed work and been appalled. I've sketched 'uglies' to illustrate criticisms only to find that when reduced to lines on a piece of paper they look very good!

Smile!

Once again the temporary notices around the county are delightful and worth looking for. You can buy fresh 'sarllards' at one greengrocer's and 'salud' at another or 'crisants' at a florist's and supermarkets have great fun trying to put the word 'trolley' into the plural!

Enquiries about modern buildings have been very fruitful:

'We don't think our building had an architect. It was put up by our company.'

'Architect! Architect! You don't think this building had an architect do you?'

'All trace of the architect's name seems to have been lost.'

'This information is not for publication'.

Guidance for disabled people

The limitations of disability are so varied and people's success at overcoming them so amazing that it's difficult to advise with any certainty.

Flights of steps, hills etc. are noted in the text. The routes round Guildford were chosen to avoid the hills. People who normally have to miss out medieval churches because of the steps down into them will find that Reigate's has no steps into it all. Otherwise it's the usual problem of kerbstones but even that's not such a problem as it used to be and some routes have been planned to take advantage of dropped kerbs. Where there was doubt the route was tested with a self-propelling wheelchair so hopefully everyone can enjoy exploring practically all of the content of this book.

Thank You

Sincere thanks are due to all the people who have opened my eyes to Surrey over the years and in particular to all the librarians, local historians, museum curators etc. who have helped further my researches. Also to the extra 'spotters' who accompanied me on field trips and especially those who put their wheelchairs round the routes.

Thanks are also due to the publishers for the opportunity to embark upon this adventure and for their encouragement to beat the developers and complete it. Keeping up with all the notes and typing was only possible with the help of Sue Harvey. To everyone concerned, thank you.

Chris Howkins
September 1990

The old crossroads at Addlestone

Addlestone

A necklace of greenery still manages to separate Addlestone from the dressing of development all around, ensuring that it remains a separate community.

ADDLESTONE MOOR
Approaching from the north side, from Chertsey or the M25, the greenery is Addlestone Moor, with one of the farms, Hatch Farm, surviving by the roundabout. (A hatch was the gateway onto common land). The rich colouring of the brickwork tells you from afar that it is 17th century. Farming, and poor farming at that, was the use of these lands for hundreds of years, ever since the district was given to Chertsey Abbey in the 7th century. Subsequent to the Dissolution of the Monasteries they were divided up into country estates.

This corner was on the edge of the 135 acre estate of Woburn. When it was purchased by Philip Southcote in about 1735, the great landscape designer William Kent was brought in and they created here a famous *ferme ornée*, an ornamental farm of which sadly little remains. The house is now part of St George's College and the beautiful grounds are but words and pictures in a book.

Woburn Hill stands though. It is the distinctive double-bowed house built in 1815 on the hilltop behind Hatch Farm, keeping its parkland image with the view up the grassy slope between mature trees to the yellow ochre walls of the house itself. It once looked out over the moor to the huddle of red roofs around the church tower that was Chertsey. Soon market gardening spread into the view but early in the 20th century the land was sold off for the housing areas that now separate the town centre from Woburn Hill.

After Hatch Farm the road humps over the railway (1848) and so past The George with its low gabled roof saying it's pre-Georgian. Inside there is timber-framing that goes back to the 16th century, making this the oldest building in the town.

HIGH STREET AND JOHN CREE

Soon you're likely to drive on to the end of the queue for the central Duke's Head traffic lights, but for compensation you might be next to a bold block of modern town houses in the High Street, opposite the Holly Tree pub. (Small holly trees were once nailed above the doors of cottages to show they were alehouses). This housing is not all new despite outward appearances. The right-hand end is the original house of John Cree the Elder, now cleaned and with additions built to match.

The Cree family were important nurserymen. John the Elder had been a plant collector in America and seems to have set up here, on his return, as a gardener at Woburn while establishing his nursery to propagate his new introductions. The nursery was certainly here by 1765 and was enlarged several times. By 1829 the catalogue offered over 5,000 different plants. At that time it was assessed as the second finest nursery in the country for rare plants.

Some of their introductions were so new to science that they had no name; thus 'nine plants unknown' were supplied for 18 shillings to their top patron. She was HRH the Princess Dowager of Wales (mother of King George III) enthusiastically building up her garden at Kew Palace, the garden that became the nucleus of the Royal Botanic Gardens, Kew.

One of the rarities she bought, for three shillings, was a weird tree that grows tooth-like projections out of its bark. In those days such similarities were believed to indicate medicinal properties for the benefit of the bodily part resembled. Hence it was a toothache tree, and is still very rare in cultivation but you'll find one a few miles away in the Savill Garden.

Between John Cree's house and the traffic lights runs the High Street – short, narrow, battered. It shows so clearly how Addlestone grew from a small community needing just a few shops, conveniently at the crossroads.

Over the lights there is still the Duke's Head pub commemorating local landowner, the Duke of York, of nursery rhyme fame (see also York Town, Camberley). This pub was the main convenience for travellers through the crossroads and remains the oldest building in the town centre.

TOWARDS THE CHURCH

West from the crossroads runs Church Road, beginning with an attractive range of Victorian tile-hung cottages.These were the only good examples left around here, prior to the gales!

Further on, Addlestone Park is now just a road, but a reminder of when the whole district was divided up into large gardens for country houses: Sayers Court, Walton Leigh, Darley Dene, Ongar Place, Coombelands and Crockford Park. Now they are just names; the houses have gone and their owners are forgotten.

A slight exception is perhaps Sayers Court which stood to the south of Church Road and was bought about 1772 as a country retreat by the architect James Paine. He is better known in the North and the Midlands, particularly for his country houses, but in the local area he designed Chertsey Bridge. His bridge over the Thames at Richmond is the more highly regarded. At first he was rather conservative but as soon as he became more adventurous so he was overtaken by the rising stardom of Robert Adam. His business went into decline and he came here, but domestic troubles caused him to retreat further – to France – and it was there that he died, in 1789.

Church Road eventually brings you to St Paul's, built in 1836 to save the people walking to Chertsey as they had done for centuries. If you want to see what an ill-proportioned duff church an architect like James Savage could produce out of London stock-brick then this is the church to see. A little explanation might help towards a greater appreciation of this building which is in fact the only one of its kind in modern Surrey.

At the beginning of the 19th century, when the population was booming, a third of the people were living in slum conditions from which Parliament deemed they needed a spiritual uplifting. Consequently they provided a million pounds for a programme of church building to be supervised by Commissioners empowered by a Church Building Act (1818). Another half million was added six years later. Most

St Paul's church, Addlestone

of the fund was spent in London but within the boundary of modern Surrey just one completely new church was funded – this one. The commissioners aimed to provide maximum capacity at the cheapest rate and that's what unfortunately shows. They were criticised at the time for their 'cheap' buildings and no doubt would have been equally criticised if they had spent a penny more than was necessary. Fortunately for the architect, James Savage, he was able to show his true talent elsewhere; his church of St Luke at Chelsea is particularly notable.

GOING SOUTH TO THE RIVER
From the Duke's Head the Brighton Road runs south towards Woking and at the beginning a few 19th century villas

remain. This was distinctly the 'up-town' end in relation to 'down-town' towards the station. My favourite building is the one with the arched carriage entrance by its side, best seen from across the street from the entrance to Burleigh Road.

Another set of traffic lights is reached before the bridge and if you turn right into Liberty Lane and then immediately left you find the car park from which a riverside walk takes you along the west bank. The river is the Bourne on its way to the Thames from its source in the great lake of Virginia Water. It is a pleasant enough walk providing you return the same way.

From the bridge you can look out over the fields of the fruit farm towards Coxes Lock Mill on the Wey Navigation. It ceased flour milling in 1982 and has been converted to residential accommodation. Formerly it worked iron and the ironmaster at one time lived in the old house in the fields. Under its stucco is timber framing. The old farm was given Dutch gables which were so Dutch that there is barely another like it in England although it is evidently of a design well used in Holland. There is no public access to it but there are public footpaths across the fields to the mill and the Pelican pub!

AMONG THE SHOPS
From the Duke's Head the road eastwards towards the station is naturally enough Station Road but outsiders are liable to think it's the High Street because this is the main shopping thoroughfare,

The tea house by the duck pond went long ago when the street was engulfed in concrete. A few older buildings survived the modernisation but gradually they have been picked off one by one. The old Co-op with its Dutch gables had a street frontage and played a part in the townscaping at a curve in the street. Now the new Royal Arsenal Co-operative Superstore has been sited so far back that it leaves a gaping great hole in the town centre, unrivalled in Surrey: a desolation of tarmacadam for cars by day and a flying school for crisp bags by night. This stunning lack of imagination is all the more unbelievable for being in the Borough of

15

Runnymede which has, on the whole, the county's best modern additions.

The rebuilding included the provision of new council offices which have now been rebuilt again. Displayed on the streetside wall is the civic heraldry of the Borough of Runnymede, a colourful reminder of the earlier history when the land was held by Chertsey Abbey, represented in the crest. Below, on the arms, is a representation of Magna Carta with the seal that was affixed to it at nearby Runnymede in 1215 by King John . His crown is shown above. Scroll, seal and crown recur on the swan supporters.

Up Crouch Oak Lane, nearly opposite, is the Baptist chapel begun in 1828. The Nonconformists were active here before the Anglicans, which is somewhat unusual, and there was once a chapel earlier than this one, as testified by Chapel Avenue, Chapel Grove and Chapel Park, although the exact location of the chapel remains unknown. It was the royal miniaturist painter Robert Bowyer who was instrumental in founding the movement here.

At the end of Crouch Oak Lane is the tree itself, an ancient boundary marker of Windsor Great Park and the oldest thing in the town. John Wycliffe who rashly supervised the translation of the Bible into English back in the 14th century is said to have preached beneath this tree. Plans in the 19th century to commemorate the event with a monument came to nothing.

A FORGOTTEN CORNER

When it was being planned to extend the residential areas of Addlestone, an alternative to the accepted western end towards Rowtown was the Weybridge end beyond the station. There was already a church there, St Augustine's, which some thought could form the nucleus of the new area. That didn't happen, which has left older parts of the town largely unaltered.

Best of all is Albert Road. Here you'll find a cul-de-sac of Victorian terraced housing showing a whole range of building materials and decorative motifs. Across the end, facing up the street is a dignified detached villa that contributes so much to the townscaping. From beside it a path goes over the river Bourne from where one William Boulton dredged the gravel to build the street. That was about 1880. The early beginnings are poorly recorded with even the name unknown for originally Albert Road was the next one, unless the map-makers made a mistake.

Having built the houses a school was needed and was duly built in 1882. A delightful little stone building that didn't close until 1982 it looks like a little church. Indeed it served that function until 1891 but was really too small; the cleric had to change in the house opposite. From 1891 there was a new church but only of corrugated iron, known as the 'tin church'. That has now been demolished and the site reused for a Mormon church (reached by the aforementioned footpath which can be taken further through the caravan park to explore the river banks and open fields of Chertsey Meads).

Ashford

A stone horse trough, uninscribed save for the date 1902, stands by the junction of Church Road and Feltham Road in the centre of Ashford. It is the most tangible echo of the town's past. It is even full of water instead of potting compost and bedding plants. Modernity stands all around yet it's interesting.

Just two statistics prepare us for the Ashford of today: the population in 1801 was just 264; it is now thought to be over 30,000. In other words, it was too small to have left many interesting old buildings and we can now expect large residential development. That is indeed the case, but another reasonable deduction will leave us disappointed. One might guess that Ashford boomed with the coming of the railway and consequently there might be some interesting Victorian terracing schemes. That is not the case, however. Ashford did develop with the railway but not into massed housing. Instead, this became a desirable 'out-of-town' location for a few big country houses set in their grounds, bright and breezy on the edge of the common.

From the horse trough you can see old cedar trees as street trees, which once shaded the lawns of such houses. The swirl of long skirts and the clunk of croquet balls are impossible to imagine; even the houses themselves have gone. Only their names survive, fossilised into flats, like 'Normanhurst' by the trough. The last survivor was 'The Elms', its name stone still embedded in the street wall.

These great houses prevented the growth of mean Victorian terraces. They held tenure over the land until they too became outdated and lost their hold. Thus, most of Ashford has been built amid cornfields and market gardens within the memory span of the older residents. It is plain ordinary and yet that very ordinariness makes it unlike anywhere else in this book and worthy of a good sociological study.

Let's begin with the greatest of these lands, the Convent, which adjoined the end of the street. Well known as a rest

Stone horse trough dated 1902, Ashford

home for a certain type of lady – the Ecclesfield Certified Inebriates Retreat – it was mostly burned down in 1921. After this the graves were exhumed and the lands developed. Their extensiveness can be appreciated by driving round the roads that made the approximate boundary: Feltham Road, Feltham Hill Road and Park Road. Cutting across the site is the later Convent Road.

The space has been used as a fairground but is now built over, save the playing fields of Echelford School and those attached to the first of the developments, St Michael's Roman Catholic School. The odd name of Echelford was the original of Ashford, the ford over the river Ash or Echel. Place names in Surrey like Esher and Eashing are also derived from ash trees.

The ford became a bridge and was sited at the southern end of Fordbridge Road. Another bridge has been added and the two looped together to make a roundabout on Staines Road West, but part of the balustrading of the oldest surviving part can still be spotted on the east side.

Another of Ashford's little peculiarities is that the aforementioned Feltham Hill Road has no hill along it. Neither has Chattern Hill. This, after all, is the flat landscape of the lower Thames valley and has no vantage points. That didn't suit the Romans of neighbouring Pontes (Staines) and so they built two look-out hills known as 'botani'. They have long since gone yet survive in today's street language.

CHURCH ROAD

Older residents will re-create for you the picture from their memories of the old village street running up to the Town Tree under which was the horse trough and beyond it the main entrance, arched in ironwork, to the Convent. That street is now Church Road but the entrance to the Convent has gone. Town Tree Road is there instead, recalling the oak that was felled in 1952 to make the present roundabout, and the trough has been moved to the side. Trees have been ancient focal points in many Surrey places, as elsewhere in the country. The borough takes its name from the spell-thorn or speaking tree where the Saxons gathered for their meetings. Sadly that too has now gone. About a dozen examples of such trees, marking the meeting place of the men of the Hundred, are known in Britain. There was a second in Surrey – Copthorn over in the eastern corner.

Setting off down the village street, there is the vicarage (1875) on the left and the church opposite. The medieval church was rebuilt in 1796. It wasn't a grand building, as in the Middle Ages there was just a tiny agricultural community here, tending the fields of their great landlord, the Abbot of Westminster. The abbey ensured development was severely restricted as was the case with Egham, Chobham and Thorpe under the Abbots of Chertsey. Even so, the Goode family became wealthy enough to be commemorated in a brass that still survives in the present church. At the Dissolution it was not the good fortune of Ashford to be freed from strict tenure. It was absorbed into the extensive lands or Honour that surrounded Hampton Court so that Henry VIII could have the fun of the chase on his doorstep. The king that had been Europe's greatest athlete was becoming fat and decrepit.

In the chancel of the medieval church was buried, in 1750, Peter Storer, Lord of the Manor and member of the Inner Temple. His tomb-slab is now stranded in the eastern churchyard because the present church was not built on the exact site of its predecessor. The dedication was changed too, from St Michael to St Matthew and when it was due for rebuilding again, in the 19th century, the plans of the noted architect, William Butterfield were changed. Thus it's not a very splendid place. A quarter of the cost came from the Welsh Charity School (now St David's girls school) and in recognition of this the range of low seating in the south aisle is reserved for them.

Here, as in no other Surrey town, it is the Roman Catholic church rather than the Anglican that makes the greatest contribution to the townscaping. Back in the 1920s a Dr Kennedy gave a prime site at the junction of Fordbridge Road with Church Road for such a provision. In 1926 fund-raising was enhanced splendidly with the opening of a fete by none other than King Manoel of Portugal. They went right to the top for their architect too, so that when building began in 1928 it was to the designs of Sir Giles Gilbert Scott who had recently designed the chapel for Charterhouse School, his other notable Surrey work (1922). Ashford's new church was dedicated to St Michael like the old parish church but building continued in stages as funds became available. Dr Kennedy's house became the Presbytery.

For a complete contrast note the old fire station next to the Royal Hart. It was opened in 1905 and looks very much of that date; much more of a feature could be made of it as they have done at Byfleet. Even in the 1920s it still had a horse-drawn engine which was not finally sold off until 1926. It sounds archaic today but shows how slowly Ashford rambled into the 20th century. When it came to putting a hard surface on the new roads the householders had to pay their share of the cost which they didn't like one bit. Their objections succeeded in reducing the width of the roadway, thereby saving themselves three shillings per foot. That's why along several roads, such as Station Crescent, the paving slabs do not reach the kerbstones and the gap has been filled with bitumen.

In other ways Ashford was quick to accept the new. A cinema, the Clarendon, opened in Clarendon Road straight after the First World War and lasted until the Second. (It is still there as the undertakers'). Then in 1939 the bigger, grander Astoria opened here in Church Road and ran until 1975 when it became the inevitable bingo hall. Its distinctive 1930s architecture is well worth keeping. So often has this style been used for cinemas that it's difficult to see it without recalling one, and Ashford has just such a case. It's a school. Formerly Echelford School, it is now the Clarendon County First School, opened in 1934. Just look at the main entrance! Preserve it!

Back in Church Road is another distinctive school, the former County Grammar School which opened in 1911 when the county was Middlesex. The county arms over the door has not been changed. The architect shrugged off the Victorian styles, save for the decoration round the main entrance, in favour of a firmly squared up central façade of seven bays, extending a further three bays each side. It is greened over with virginia creeper in summer and now goes under the title of Spelthorne College.

Look down beyond the left end to the distant roof and you'll see a giant 'V' in brighter red tiles. That's the victory 'V' inserted at the end of the Second World War. Among the former pupils was Irene Thomas. Remember her on *Brain of Britain* and *Round Britain Quiz*?

Finally, before the railway, is the Post Office; small and smart in large red bricks, a pseudo-classical building with distinctive white urns on either end of the front parapet, just like the one in Staines. This, too, needs keeping when there are so few good buildings in Ashford.

Over the railway is St David's girls school, formerly the Welsh Charity School for Boys and Girls, opened by Prince Albert in 1857. He arrived by special train, necessitating a rapid refurbishing of the little station, but nothing of that remains. For their centenary in 1957 it was Princess Margaret's turn to visit and she was much taken by their full length statuette of Prince Albert that he had presented on the occasion of his visit.

Henry Clutton's imposing buildings were a new home for a school that was already in existence, having been founded in Clerkenwell in 1718 by the Honourable and Loyal Society of Ancient Britons (the London Welshmen). Pupils had to have been born within twelve miles of the Royal Exchange and to have at least one parent who was Welsh. The school's story is all very interesting but the important point is the stamp of acceptance and respectability its presence gave to Ashford. Other institutions followed, such as the almshouses over in Feltham Hill Road.

The almshouses are not great architecture but a valuable part of Ashford's heritage nevertheless, and were refurbished 1986-1987. A clear inscription, visible from the road, relates that these are the Rowland Hill Almshouses, founded in Hill Street, Blackfriars Road, London in 1811, while the right-hand block declares its connection with Christ Church, Westminster Bridge, and was removed here in 1894. The preacher in that church was the Rowland Hill hereby commemorated. Another block, over to the right is inscribed over its street door, 'Vaughan Almshouses. Founded in Southwark 1866. Removed here 1907.'

That was when the horse trough was new, when the landscape was richly treed with orchards and the new golf club was being created out in the farmlands that were being sold off to developers. The clubhouse had been the old manor house going back to the days when this was the edge of the wild wastes of Hounslow Heath, notorious for highwaymen. That hasn't changed as much as the landscape – in the 1960s the captain of the golf club was jailed for helping to mastermind an armed bank raid!

Camberley & Frimley

Camberley is the white elephant town. There by the A30 stands a large tubular white elephant created by a pipe-making firm on the adjoining site. The firm have moved on

Camberley's white elephant

but their prodigy remains, the conspicuous landmark used by locals when giving directions in this busy modern town.

THE FOUNDATION OF THE TOWN
As heavy traffic rumbles down the A30 on the edge of Camberley, so once the stage-coaches ran this way and galloping alongside them some of the country's most notorious highwaymen. There was William Davis who paid his bills in gold 'The Golden Farmer', and then there was also the sinful curate of Yateley, Parson Darby (hence Darby Green) and the most famous of the bunch, the Frenchman, Claude Duval. One even victimised the hated Judge Jeffreys. None of them had to worry about Camberley though – it did not exist.

At that time the local centre of population was the ancient village of Bagshot to the south. All around was the desolation of Bagshot Heath, as attractive to highwaymen as was Hounslow Heath to the north. Bagshot itself was doing well under the patronage of the stage-coaches but since Norman times it had been known for something else, the Royal Park, hence the stag's head on the Borough's armorial bearings.

Thus it was that George III came to review his troops on Bagshot Heath in 1792. That opened some people's eyes to the potential of this area for military purposes and in so doing made the first step towards the founding of modern Camberley.

First to move into the wilderness was the Royal Military College, now the Academy, known all over the world from its location just over the Berkshire border as Sandhurst. It was transferred from Marlow in 1799, in the hope that the wilderness would offer fewer distractions to the innocent young men. Some hopes! People from Marlow and Wycombe, especially the traders, packed their things and followed on.

When, in 1812, the college opened on a new site, given to the Government by Prime Minister Pitt, so the camp followers set up shop outside the gates. Naturally enough this became known as New Town. Its name was changed to York Town in 1838 to honour the man who laid the foundation stone of the college, the Commander-in-Chief of the army, the Duke of York (of nursery rhyme fame).

By 1851, when there were just five houses in Park Street, this community was sufficiently confident to commission St Michael's church. Their chosen architect was the young Henry Woodyer. He had only recently (in 1847) finished his first church, St Mark's, Whyke (see *Hidden Surrey*) and his church at York Town, with its fine townscape value, already gives indications of the qualities to come (see Dorking). The population of the whole district was still less than 2,000.

The name of York Town persists in the modern town today. On the north side is the second great influential institution, the Staff College, originally the senior department of the Royal Military College, transferred from Marlow in 1820. Thus the two colleges belong to the same institution, sometimes causing considerable confusion. Later the Duke of Cambridge laid the foundation stone for new buildings and these were ready for their official opening by Prince Albert in 1862. It was always said that standing in the rain watching the workmen was what gave the Prince his fatal chill, whereas the story nowadays is that he caught typhoid at Windsor.

Once again a little town began to grow up around the new college. This one was named Cambridge Town after the founder. With the coming of the railways this caused confusion with the university town and a change of name was called for and officially sanctioned. The new name was compounded from local elements: the river Cam + Amber hill + ley for a field. Whereas York Town has persisted, Cambridge Town has not.

It is refreshing to explore the beginnings of a Surrey new town without getting involved in railways, but with something as different as the two branches of the Royal Military College. The crucial influence of both the junior department at Sandhurst and the senior department at Camberley is commemorated on the Borough's arms. There you'll find the crossed swords of the army badge. You'll also find the sinister (left) supporter is a white owl. That is taken from the Le Marchant's bearings who were baronets of Chobham. Lieutenant Colonel John Gaspard Le Marchant founded the two colleges and became first Lieutenant-Governor, to teach the lessons learnt from the Crimean War and to replace fallen officers.

The Staff College has its own museum which can be viewed by appointment. Bagshot Park, from where George III started all this, is also used by the army and houses the museum of the Royal Army Chaplains Department (viewing by appointment). (For Surrey's three other military museums and the Red Cross museum see the Museums' Council's leaflet at a library, museum or council offices.)

THE NEW TOWN

From the college gates to the landscape value of the church spire, from bits of early housing to the little shops that served them, there are fragments of the story dotted around to illustrate the development. It must be admitted though that modern Camberley is just that – modern.

Readers may find the fringes more rewarding for the many examples of the larger houses that still survive there; the sort outsiders tend to call 'posh' but which Surrey folk barely notice because they are so much a part of the county scene. These particular examples belonged to a different social group: senior staff and retired officers from the Army, retaining their links with the district. Many military people with familiar names have had connections with Camberley, with Churchill and Montgomery heading the list. A lesser known personage was Grace Reynolds who founded the Royal Cadet Corps and is commemorated here by Grace Reynolds' Walk.

As implied, not all of old Camberley was built on a grand level. There were narrow streets of Victorian terraces and shops as in other Surrey towns. The bandmaster at Sandhurst, for example, lived in York Town and sent his son to the local school. That was little Arthur Sullivan who shared his father's love of music and grew up to fame in the partnership we simply call 'Gilbert and Sullivan'.

The shopkeepers had a very mixed society to serve. Needing to gather their takings from whomever they could, they stocked cheap goods but also strove to please their so-called better customers and didn't fail to advertise the fact. Traviss Bros, ironmongers, advertised 'By Appointment to the Royal Military College', while J Sworder, fruiterer, could go one better with 'By Appointment to HRH The Duke of Connaught, the Royal Military College and Staff Colleges, etc'. Similarly we don't find the cobblers bothering to advertise their ordinary work boots but riding boots and, for those leisurely Edwardian afternoons in large summer gardens, 'tennis shoes in great varieties'.

Social connections had been greatly enhanced by the building of the railway link in 1887 and then, too, the more wealthy people could move out of London to enjoy Camberley's other great asset, its country air, fragrant with pines from Bagshot Heath. As early as 1873 no less a publication then *The Lancet* was extolling the virtues of Camberley air and so, in 1899, it was chosen by Brompton

Hospital as the site for its country sanatorium for consumptive patients. An estate agent's advertisement, now displayed in the town museum, says it all:

'CAMBERLEY– the Rising Residential Health Resort, about one hour from London. Approached by two lines of railway from Waterloo.'

The expansion was possible because the district was open parkland, Frimley Park. There had been a park house of sorts since the 1600s but the present mansion, used as Frimley Park Hospital, was not built until 1760. A hundred years later it was owned by Captain Charles Raleigh Knight and it was he who began the building programme with Park Road, Park Street, and High Street. He could certainly spare the land. His park covered more than nine square miles.

The best house in Camberley is down the southern end of Park Road, beyond the railway. It was built by Surrey's greatest architect, Sir Edwin Lutyens, the man who could be monumental on both a grand scale and a small one like this; the man who could use traditional materials without looking old-fashioned. This beautifully kept house looks so modern yet it is Victorian, built in 1898. Sadly the Gertrude Jekyll garden that went with it has not survived.

The town has been growing ever since, especially with the opening of the M3 in 1972. Now it has a population of some 78,000 and looks much as any other town in the country and just as busy. Explorers should heed the Borough motto, Festina Diligenter – make haste carefully!

FRIMLEY

Frimley and Frimley Green lie to the south of Camberley but are rapidly merging into one. This was heathland belonging to Chertsey Abbey with a limited and poor peasant economy. Things didn't improve when it was emparked.

The district wasn't even very supportive of the usual craftsmen; miles of heathland and yet only two broom-makers in the 1841 census. Around here they were called broom bashers or dashers, whereas over in the heathlands of the Wey Valley they were broom squarers or squires. A broom dasher scene has been reconstructed in Camberley Museum.

The most rewarding part here is the Basingstoke Canal to the south. It was in 1796 that the canal was opened, running some 34 miles from the Hampshire heartland to join the Wey Navigation at New Haw and thence to the Thames and the London markets. That journey became impossible in the 20th century due to dereliction but now, after many years of tremendous effort, they are putting the finishing touches to its restoration and it is hoped that it will be fully operational once again soon. The towpath is the place to resort when you've had enough of exploring Camberley and Frimley. There you can enjoy its beautiful woodland setting and walk out through countryside as far as you wish.

Caterham

This is chalk downland country. Over in the west it runs as the narrow spine of the Hog's Back, to become the wall of scarp faces along the Vale of Holmsdale and then, after Reigate, it broadens out into this high rolling plateau so deeply cut with coombes.

Up on the airy downs a scattering of fascinating ancient churches testify to man's long habitation in poor farming communities, like Chelsham, Chaldon and Farleigh. Then the railways brought fresh development, with places like Woldingham turning the Downs into a garden suburb. Exploring round here is liable to take you through Caterham.

In fact there are two Caterhams and they could not be more different. As with the aforementioned villages, the first settlement was up on the downs and is known as Caterham-on-the-Hill. Then the railways came running through the valley below and spawned a new settlement, known as Caterham-in-the-Valley. Neither has much to draw visitors from afar but the locals find this area as absorbing as anywhere else and indeed its local history group, The Bourne Society is the largest in the country. Their publications in the museum in the Valley centre will guide visitors with special interests.

A railway to Caterham was proposed in 1854 as 'a great public and local advantage' which is rather unbelievable when there were only about a dozen households from which to recoup the massive outlay. To the south, however, were important stone quarries. These, as it happened, never brought financial success to the railway. Some of the later schemes were not even attempted.

More entertaining is the story of the buses which began life far away in Hastings in 1901. There they failed in competition with the electric trams and mouldered away until 1907 when the fleet set off to begin life again in London. Alas they were past it. Two eventually got as far as Caterham and here they stayed, one stripped to provide spare parts for the other. This was put into service between Caterham and Godstone by a couple of enterprising drivers. Whoops! They had no licence from the Metropolitan Police and that was the end of that – until 1914 when a new authorised service began.

By then there had been much building and rebuilding in the Valley. Today little remains of the early township but drive up the hill to step back into the Middle Ages.

Church Hill used to be even steeper (poor carriage horses!) and was the driveway to the court next to the old church of St Lawrence. This was built at the end of the 11th century and remained in use until it failed to fulfil Victorian expectations. They built a new church of St Mary opposite and closed the old one, thus allowing it to be one of the few Surrey churches to escape 19th century restoration.

The church is interesting as soon as you step off the hill. There in the south wall a break in the masonry shows clearly that the Normans built a little church with a rounded apse at the east end rather than the present square chancel. Then the wall shows blocked arches which once led from the church into a south aisle or chapels, now gone.

Step inside and the pews have gone, to leave a lovely open space just as there would always have been in pre-Reformation days. Now we can stand or kneel in this space by the chancel step just as the medieval worshippers did for their services. Parts of the basal dado of the chancel screen remain to remind us that this was as far east as the congregation was permitted. Above would have been the focal point, the great rood, and the roof beam is still scarred with notches from its provision. The walls are still reddened from the wall paintings and the capitals still carry their foliage sculpture – that on the northern side is most unusual, that in the south chancel wall is embellished with a little face.

The sculptured face you cannot miss greets you on entering. Hands pull the corners of the mouth wide apart as in warnings to gossips that there is no Christian virtue in being a big-mouth, but as this head is adorned with pig-like ears it is more likely a warning against one of the Seven Deadly Sins – gluttony.

A more serene face in white marble was provided by a sculptor on the monument to his mother, Elizabeth Legrew. Opposite is the inscribed stone to John Lambert, who was

Yeoman to His Majesty's Chamber but that's not so easy to read as the mason managed to miss out some of the letters. We should not presume he was literate. He probably followed a master-copy and made mistakes. Then, or later, someone scratched in corrections to his errors. Lambert's own downfall was his loyalty to his king, Charles I. That made him a threat to the Parliamentarians so they curbed him by seizing most of his lands.

Beautiful downland still survives all around, on this outer fringe of Greater London. The former London Corporation boundary markers are still strung through the district. An easy one to find is beside Coulsdon Road opposite The Grove, on the present boundary line.

To the north lies Whyteleafe with little of great interest and to the north-east, Warlingham, trying to retain its village character and with a few old buildings. The church is best, with its medieval mural of St Christopher and a modern window recording the tradition that here came Archbishop Cranmer to hear the first reading of the new Prayer Book in English that he had written (in part at Chertsey, in the redundant abbey outbuildings). Free of unintelligible Latin, the Faith came to the people and appropriately, hundreds of years later, from here came the first church service to be televised.

Chertsey

~

THE OLD CENTRE

Don't look for the High Street. Chertsey doesn't have one – it has been called Windsor Street since the late 18th century. At its junction with Guildford Street and London Street you're in the 'town centre' but what a centre!

Look around and there is very little that has changed since the 1950s; little has changed in fact since the early years of the 20th century. It is not entirely a Victorian centre either for there are lots of buildings in all three directions that are 18th century or even older with brick façades from that time. It is not of the finest Georgian architecture so it attracts none of the attention that Castle Street in Farnham receives, which is

The Cedars, Windsor Street in Chertsey

a pity, for the everyday solutions to building needs and problems that have been solved here are every bit as exciting. What is more, thanks to the researches of the museum and some keen local historians, something is known about the people who have lived in practically every old building in the town. Much of it is, of course, of purely local interest but there are some good tales to tell and from them we do get a colourful picture of the past, so let us look at this centre a little more closely.

Firstly, Windsor Street broadens noticeably at this junction, wide enough for market stalls on a Saturday, which is a nice continuity for this has been the market place since 1282. The original charter somehow became invalid so that in 1588/9 the county agents for Elizabeth I 'credibly informed' her that it would be 'a great relief' to the 'inhabitants of the said village' if they received a 'Royal grant and ordinance' for the holding of markets again and for a grant of land on which to build a market hall. That was forthcoming and the hall very rapidly constructed – a room upon wooden pillars to create a covered market space beneath.

There is a painting of it in the museum but the hall has gone and in quite a spectacular way. It was attracting rowdies who disrupted the church services early in the 19th century and was further condemned as an eyesore in front of the newly restored church. The arguments continued until one John Brown decided to harness a horse team to the end pillars and haul the lot down! Oh, he cleared up the mess. In fact he sold it off and landed in court, accused of selling the materials at transactions out of town so that nobody knew exactly how much he got or, more to their point, how much went into his own pocket!

A little to the east is the Crown Inn and it was the landlord here who came to the rescue. He provided some adjoining land for a new market hall away from the front of the church. Very generous you might think, but there was the small matter of a connecting door between the market hall and the pub – only for the convenience of people wanting to come in out of the cold you understand!

That hall only lasted until 1851-2 when the present Town Hall was built – clear of the pub you'll notice. The market beneath this hall was commercially unsuccessful and the room above proved inadequate for the County Courts and Magistrates Courts that sat there. To here came the case over the last duel fought in England, over Englefield Green way. Then in 1922 civic pride fell to an all time low with the Council leasing the property for the provision of public lavatories.

Notice the very smart Georgian houses adjoining the other side of the Town Hall. In their humble way they are some of the nicest in the town. Built about 1780, stuccoed sometime in the 19th century, these were the premises acquired by two local businessmen for starting the Chertsey Bank, hence Old Bank House. They were George and Thomas La Coste, Chertsey's millers and wharfingers. George lived here while Thomas lived in the mill house of Abbey Mill. Their bank functioned from 1815 until George's death in about 1847 when the bank moved into the next pair of houses, also stuccoed, and continued until 1877. Meanwhile Bank House became the home of Dr C J Eady whose son, Sir Charles, became Master of the Rolls. On being raised to the peerage in 1919 he took the title Baron Swinfen of Chertsey. Notice the stately yet restrained little porch to the house which was evidently added to give that little touch of dignity appropriate for a bank.

The Crown was an important coaching inn, prosperous enough for rebuilding on its present large scale in 1899. The stable blocks behind were swept away to make the car park. Next door, appropriately enough, was the smithy, but in 1890 the present three-storey block was built on the site. Look carefully at its frontage and you'll see it still records being the showroom for the coaches and carriages built by Charles Head & Sons. Charles Head arrived in the town in 1863, aged about 30 but with an eye to the future. In 1871 he was recorded as a coachpainter. A factory site was acquired at 25 Station Road. Other premises were owned in Kensington and Woking. Still the family pressed on and had a petrol pump installed in 1904. They proudly advertised that they could build cars to any design.

Next door is another business linking the days of hand craftsmen with those of mass production. It is a chain store

The Surplus Stores outside Chertsey railway station

for furnishings which had previously been a cabinet makers'. When many of the town's Georgian houses were new, at the end of the 18th century, two Sparrows worked here to make the furniture. They were an uncle and nephew, both named Joseph. Uncle lived until about 1823 and some three years after that the nephew sold out to Claud Waterer who came from Walton but belonged to the more famous Woking family of that name. He extended his business to include that of estate agent, which still continues today. The cabinet-making workshops were round the back, reached by a side path now converted for public use as Church Walk. The irregular roof line of this block results from the third storey having to be dismantled after a fire.

That brings us to the church which is largely Church-warden Gothic and not one of the great town churches of Surrey. The crown-post roof in the chancel is worth a look and on the step of the south chapel are some examples (poor) of the famous Chertsey tiles (see museum display). Most intriguing is a sculptured stone corbel up above the high altar. It might be medieval and there is little of that in Surrey. It might perhaps have come from the abbey because this is unlikely to have been its original position; medieval symbolism reserved this area for representing God enthroned, with the Church elders about him. This sculpture is a grotesque. His buttoned tunic suggests he might be a cleric but why he's covering part of his face with one hand is lost on us today.

When the church was almost rebuilt early in the 19th century, the authorities thought it prudent to write into the contract that no fee would be paid until the contractor had completed the roof. Little did they imagine that he would frame up an open structure of beams, put a roof on it, take his money and skip the country! Chertsey was none too pleased at having to pay another contractor to come and build the walls. One did, and the beams are still concealed inside those walls today.

Outside is a gem of Victoriana. It is a beautifully designed water pump and basin. It is so very Victorian, showing off style, new industrialism, purposefulness, self-esteem; all cast solid in iron. It was presented in 1863 by John Pratt Briscoe with one of those public spirited gestures that we would expect of the man who became MP for North-West Surrey, who built his country estate of Foxhills to the south (now a country club and golf course) and who married a daughter of Sir Joseph Mawbey of adjoining Botleys Park (now used by the National Health Service).

While in the area listen for Chertsey's unusual church clock. After the church clock strikes 8.00pm a bell tolls a further 50 times (about two minutes) and then swing chimes once for each day of the month ie 16 times on the 16th, between Michaelmas and Lady Day. It is perpetuating the ancient custom of ringing the curfew.

and Guildford Street, is a large building, recently rebuilt with the design of the street façade replicated. It has been Cross and Herbert's chemist and pharmacy since right back in the early years of the 19th century. What a tradition! The most notable pharmacist was A W Gerrard who arrived in 1843. He is the Gerrard of Cuxson-Gerrard Chemicals who, among other things, made adhesive plasters. The company has since been absorbed into ICI. He is also of note locally for having installed an electricity generator into a warehouse behind the shop from which he provided the town's first electric light.

The son of another pharmacist was the writer Albert Smith who lived at 13 Windsor Street. That was part of an important 18th century block opposite the church but was unfortunately gutted by fire in 1987. The original frontages were due to be saved when the rest of the structure had to be dismantled, but the whole lot was flattened. It was thanks to Albert Smith that we have the story of Blanche Heriot and the curfew bell. It was thanks to one of his friends, Charles Dickens, that Chertsey features in *Oliver Twist*.

The incident concerns a robbery and the details are recognisable as those of a real robbery that was perpetrated at the back of Gogmore Lane. It was in that lane that Smith went to live and where Dickens visited him. Until recently it was possible to retrace the villains' footsteps but now the whole area is due for demolition and redevelopment. Not only will Chertsey have lost both the homes of Albert Smith, but the second was also lived in by an even better known Victorian writer, Thomas Love Peacock.

HERIOT ROAD AND THE NEW DEVELOPMENT BY THE CAR PARKS
While the neighbouring town centres – Walton, Addlestone, Woking, Staines – were being redeveloped, that at Chertsey remained dormant with small shops and family businesses. When the new centres attracted customers away, Chertsey decayed. By the late 1970s traders were successful in demanding a face-lift for the town and it is now a much more attractive place to visit.

New development has been allowed beside Heriot Road which now takes traffic from the old town hall round behind the old centre into Guildford Street, relieving upper Guildford Street of much of its congestion. It is now an 'Access Only' thoroughfare but thoroughfare it still is, so it

Eighteenth century houses in Windsor Street, Chertsey

remains alive and vital, in a way that would not have been so if plans to exclude traffic completely had been effected.

Heriot Road takes its name from Blanche Heriot of local legend. Her lover was due to be hanged at the ringing of the curfew bell so she clung to the clapper to deaden the sound. It deadened her too. It has not been possible to substantiate any part of this legend. The medieval manor of Beomonds, which was on the site of the Victorian school at the end of Windsor Street, is perpetuated here, too, as the name of the new housing which was the first of the modern developments. Being end-on to the road they create variety and better townscaping by contrasting with Waverley House that has been built a little further up with a long street frontage. Opposite is the Sainsbury's centre, playing an important note by repeating the use of red brick and slate of Beomonds and of the local tradition – the old town hall at the top is of brick and slate too. At the bottom the same pattern continues, first with Chertsey Hall and then some later additions. It is not monotonous though. Architects have had freedom to express their individualism while restraining themselves to low levels, interesting surfaces, brick, slate and tile. It is some of the best recent townscaping in the county.

Cranleigh

Rooks cawing in the high trees behind the old parish church amid the tiled roofs of village cottages and the green fields and woods beyond – what a clichéd picture of England. At Cranleigh it is true!

The largest village in England, they claim, and when the Guildford Road hurls you suddenly out of the trees onto the open common and village green you do feel that you've arrived somewhere. The fringe of brick and tile cottages, many from the 16th and 17th centuries, standing as patient spectators, look quite diminutive across the grass. What grass it is too, proudly defeating all rival claimants to be rated the second finest cricket pitch after the Oval. Many a famous player has been to test it, or be tested by it, and even to live beside it.

Cricket on a village green is, of course, a rarity since the motoring age proved windscreens and cricket balls are incompatible. Here they play on – the green is so big. (The largest in England is not here but is still in Surrey, at Ripley, where they can play at cricket well clear of the road).

Beside the green is the first sign that Cranleigh must be populous – a cinema. Built by the local unemployed in 1936, The Regal still operates as a cinema and not a bingo hall, so one is full of expectations for quite a sizable place.

Most intriguing is the way the green continues as a long, long wide finger beside the road, between the houses, right into the heart. It is avenued with the splendid red-leaved *Acer* schwerdern, now mature and stately and a rare sight. When it ends you're in the centre. Another 400 yards and you're out. Cranleigh isn't big at all.

ALONG THE HIGH STREET

The cinema by the Green is not the only thing that hints at township here. The centre has a modern shopping area, tastefully set back from the old building line to create a little plaza. With coloured paving, formal planters and a fountain it is all very town-like. It is well done too and just proves that not all work from the 1960s is best hurried past. It is not only good in itself but in the way it adds harmoniously to the village.

It has a little surprise, too. Follow the service road round the right-hand end to the back. You'll find it drops lower to enable direct unloading onto a platform – and that's exactly what it is – the platform of the former railway station. Just to prove it, there at the beginning you can still see the bracket steps in the facing where the railway staff crossed the line. The line opened in 1865 and was closed down under the Beeching Plan just a few months before it was able to celebrate its centenary.

From the plaza your eye is likely to be caught by the colonnaded building in the central reservation. It's a rather grand drinking fountain erected as a memorial in 1889 (see plaque). Big and bold, of local stone with a local Horsham slab stone roof, it looks well in today's scene but rather incongruous in old photos with a cattle market all around it!

It was the gift of a member of the family at nearby Knowle. Several great estates, such as Baynards and Vachery, have all played their part in Cranleigh's local history. At Vachery, for example, there has been a lake for hundreds of years, which was enlarged to about 100 acres as an upper reservoir to water the Wey Arun Junction Canal. There should have been two such reservoirs but landowners prevented the other being built and thereby hastened the canal's failure. It was prone to running out of water because this area was higher than either end. Centuries before this, wild cranes used it and gave their name to Cranleigh. There is one carved on top of the drinking fountain to remind us.

Knowle, in 1657, hosted none other than the great Oliver Cromwell, in return for which he granted Cranleigh two fairs a year. His men were billeted in the village in what was then a newish building, now called Cromwell House. It has become one of the grand old houses in the street, delightfully informal and always cheery in red brick and tile, with splendid hand-made tiles on the walls. Just compare these with the affront of massed machine-made tiles on the street face of the public library over the road. You can see part of the inside of Cromwell House because it is a restaurant, or

The Cottage Hospital at Cranleigh

you can take coffee in the front garden and watch the world go by. Cranleigh's best when it's busy. Hopefully that will distract you from the supermarket opposite. How could a planning committee allow such a building here?

Behind it, beside the car park, is an even uglier building with a corrugated iron roof. It is interesting. It has no windows and has odd panels in the roof. This was the Central Cinema, opened in 1910, and one of Surrey's few surviving early ones (see Godalming). It continued to function until 1935 when it was condemned as a fire hazard, after which the aforementioned Regal was built.

Back in the street you may well notice Barclays Bank for its smart little classical design. There are differences and contrasts all along the way, spanning 500 years, from half-timbering of the 16th century to sensitive recent work like that on the junction with Knowle Lane. Somehow it all fits together into an acceptable whole.

More subtle than the building styles are their usages. The little shops have always served a wide and predominantly agricultural area with everyday needs and this still persists today. Traditions that have been fast disappearing elsewhere, like fresh meat butchers' shops. There is William Dyer's, complete with decorative glazed wall tiles and sawdust on the floor, next door to an even greater rarity – the fresh fish shop – and over the road another butcher's. No supermarket has ousted these.

Several local families continue their tradition of long service, such as the Mann family. They started up a little ironmonger's shop in 1887 and you can still see their name in the street. Many changes have occurred of course but there is little risk of confusing the imitation with the genuine in Cranleigh. There is the 1930s love of mock timbering, for example, with the Village Hall of 1933 offering a great gable of it to the road, but with other timbering around it is acceptable. It clearly announces 1930s but doesn't shout. Another quiet but even more important building is a little further along. It is the hospital.

You'll see the sign but maybe not recognise the building. It is the very picturesque little 16th century cottage set back a little. It only became a hospital in 1859 but that made it the very first cottage hospital in the country. How amazing that something so valued today as health care should not be catered for in this way until as recently as 1859.

Even more recent and equally impressive is the social amenity centre that has been developed nearby. Not only is there the usual recreation hall but with it a more unusual grouping of separate buildings for the Scouts, Guides, Parish Council offices and, at a discreet distance, the band room. All set in grass amid trees, they make a scene worth considering elsewhere. Then there's the petrol filling station. You can't get much more modern than that idea but don't scurry past for here's another of Cranleigh's odd surprises. The main building has been adapted from an ancient timber-framed farmhouse. Does any filling-station in Surrey have an older building?

The end of the High Street is marked by a stone obelisk erected to commemorate the opening of this route as part of the London to Brighton turnpike in 1794. It acts as a grandiose milestone but you might think 'Windsor 31' is an odd destination on it. It will make more sense if you picture the Prince Regent rattling home from his Pavilion at Brighton. If you want a less romantic vision, then picture the poor wretches from the workhouse on the common being brought out here for stone breaking to maintain the turnpike.

The obelisk was set up by the local practitioner, Dr Ellery. It was his partner, Dr Napper, together with the rector, Archdeacon John Henry Sapte, who started the cottage hospital. Dr Napper served Cranleigh for 54 years, the rector, 60 years. Ellery's lasting memorial is the church porch, built by Henry Woodyer. The church is worth a visit.

THE PARISH CHURCH

The lychgate of 1880 is a rather grand structure of stone. Decide for yourself whether the stone ribs supporting a timber roof are 'admirable' or 'incongruous'. Sadly it is paved with 18th century headstones and there aren't enough of those in Surrey for any to be ground away underfoot. The more stealthy feet of the notorious Surrey/Sussex smugglers came here to hide their contraband among the graves. Some of the burials are recorded on markers of iron instead of stone. They were cast in the foundry of Filmer and Mason in Guildford (the site was redeveloped as the Yvonne Arnaud Theatre). Such markers are found in only a few other Surrey churchyards and need preserving as less familiar illustrations of the amazing Victorian rituals centred upon the deceased.

Cast iron markers were less expensive than lettered stone, but cheaper still was a painted wooden board running the length of the grave. Most of these have rotted away. Not only has one survived here but it has been restored so that once again we can read its two long lines of inscription:

'Great God in whom we live Prepare us for that day
Help us to turn to Thee to Watch and Wait and Pray.'

Towering above all this is a massive cedar of Lebanon, looking for all the world as though it has been here hundreds of years. However, it was planted only in 1863, by the Archdeacon after his honeymoon. Apparently the seedling was brought from the tree's original homeland in the Lebanon in 1846. It makes the church tower look small.

Inside it is a fine big church full of light, since a flying bomb divested it of much of the stained glass in 1944. The delicate reticulated tracery of the east window is now filled with clear glass through which, in spring, you can see the cherry blossom outside – the Japanese symbol of the resurrection.

The resurrection is permanently portrayed on a medieval brass on the north wall of the sanctuary. It is one of only two biblical scenes so engraved in Britain (the other, a nativity, is also in Surrey, at Cobham). Its subject and its position on a tomb suggests this was all part of an Easter sepulchre. The tomb is that of Robert Harding, Master of the Goldsmiths' Company in 1489.

In the north aisle on the eastern pier is the famous cat's head corbel that is reputed to have inspired Lewis Carroll's Cheshire Cat. The pier itself, and its partner to the south are quite intriguing as they carry no arch over the nave. Either the ideas were not finished or the arch was dismantled. It all looks like the crossing for a central tower that isn't there. Perhaps one was removed when the church was altered and enlarged about 1330 and rebuilt as the present west tower.

As you wander around have a look at the Victorian pulpit where you will find carved panels from a medieval screen incorporated, and also part of the floral cresting from off the bressummer. A complete but plain medieval screen still stands across the south transept.

In the floor at the western end of the nave is a black memorial slab to John Mower who died in 1716. He is the man to whom is attributed the realisation that lime makes good fertilizer for certain plants. Another memorial, on the south wall, is a wooden cross brought from the Flanders fields to become the chapel cross for Godalming's TocH. It is being cared for here until such time as they have a use for it again.

Finally, an oddity from the Nonconformists. When their chapel (of 1828) on the common was put up for sale in 1987, the estate agent's advertisement made startling reading: the lease was for 'a term of 2000 years at a yearly rent of one red rose if demanded'.

Dorking

Think big to enjoy this medieval market town; it is not the place to be overwhelmed with little details.

Best of all is the setting. From up on the North Downs at Ranmore there are expansive views down into a broad vale with the town laid out before you and the richly wooded Leith Hill range rising up beyond, tilting various parts of the town into the sun. Islanded in the trees, the town looks compact, composed of masses of tile and slate roofs unbroken by stark flat-topped blocks of modernity. It all looks so cosy and inviting and as the sun lowers, so the contrasting tones of light and shady roof pitches pucker into a rich texture all around the tall, pale spire of St Martin's in the centre.

From here you see practically all, whereas the famous view from Box Hill, a little to the east, shows more of the hills slipping down into the great blue expanse of the Weald and the great farmlands of Surrey. Dorking became its market centre. Even in late Saxon times it was valuable enough to be a possession of Queen Edith, wife of Edward the Confessor.

From this richly wooded landscape came the charcoal and firewood for London and other developing centres like Kingston. Certainly by 1329 Kingston was buying its fuel from here and continued to do so, but in 1562 was complaining about inflation. The price of a load of charcoal rose from three shillings to twenty shillings, reflecting the demands being made upon the industry by the furnaces of the Wealden iron industry.

Approach from the south and it is the same wooded hilly journey. The housing estates lie hidden out here, leaving the town compact. At the beginning of the 19th century one of the 'main roads' into Sussex via Coldharbour cut so narrowly through the hills that coffin bearers had to walk in single file with the coffin slung on a pole between them. Today the main Sussex road (A24) cuts more widely through the hills but not into the town any more. Instead you arrive at a roundabout at the east end of the main thoroughfare.

From here, one immensely long street takes you through to

the little roundabout at the western end, changing its name as it goes: Reigate Road, High Street, The Quadrant, West Street. It is continuous, gently rising and falling and changing its bearing from time to time so that just when you think you've reached the end there is a little bit more, until suddenly you're back in the trees on the Guildford side. It can surely claim to be the longest shopping street in Surrey. It is certainly delightfully old-fashioned. Small shops still predominate, like at Cranleigh, but here the scale is so much larger and there is more room for larger modern buildings.

Approach from the west along the A25 from Guildford and you are filled with anticipation as the fine spire of St Martin's punctuates the cleft in the trees and lures you onward towards a still unseen Dorking. Without it Dorking just wouldn't be the same. It is the work of that notable Victorian architect, Henry Woodyer, who did a lot of work in Surrey and St Martin's is his best. He could be just as good with little village churches, such as Buckland nearby and Hascombe which has just had its wall paintings restored so is particularly worth a visit for comparison.

THE MAIN STREET
Continue thinking big to enjoy the town in broad views rather than look for little details. What you will find is the same varied assortment of buildings from the last 400 years or so, all shoulder to shoulder, like Reigate or Cranleigh. Here there are far more attractive peeps to the downs and through to other parts of town, strung together into an impressive townscape as the street loops along.

The interest in Dorking does not centre upon any collection of fine old buildings but upon the fact that there isn't one. The old and redundant have been removed and replaced, for generation after generation, as the town has continued to regenerate itself. Half-timbered, tile-hung Tudor shoulders Georgian and Victorian in a glorious muddle. Down at shop-front level it may seem rather regular, but look up above and there is a restless interlocking of gables and roofs, dormers and sashes, stucco and brick, tile-hanging and plaster. It generates the essence of a town – that it is alive. Rather like Cranleigh, it is best viewed during shopping hours.

The process is still continuing. Recent infills occur at regular intervals but mostly fit their setting visually as well as physically. There was, recently, a notice informing people that the redevelopment of a site would preserve the old façade when in fact there was nothing but a desolation of rubble there! The significant modern developments are all grouped out of town by the station beside the Leatherhead road where they create no conflict with the fine old centre. In the High Street one good example is the Trustee Savings Bank/Halifax Building Society block which has an appropriate scale and is carefully set back behind planters, and has an irregular gabled roof line in the Dorking spirit. Nearby, in complete contrast, are a couple of reminders of 18th century days. Number 225 and 227 remain as street houses without the addition of ground floor shop fronts, one in red brick with iron railing, the other cream with stucco.

The one building that catches most people's eye is the White Hart, formerly Cross House from the heraldic cross of the Knights of the Order of St John who were earlier holders of the site. The coaching inns and pubs of Dorking have bred much speculation as to which inspired Charles Dickens to bring Tom Weller and Sam here in *Pickwick Papers*. Dickens himself is considered by some to have contributed the unsigned assertion in *All the Year Round* that it was The King's Head. That building no longer stands but was at the junction of South Street and High Street where the bank stands today.

That bank contributes quite smartly to the junction when viewed from the end of West Street. To the right is Chitty's the butcher's, founded right back in 1800 and still outdoing the supermarkets. In Dorking you can still go shopping in the traditional way, even in the High Street, where high rents and rates have so often squeezed out small businesses in other towns, to be replaced by services, such as estate agents and insurance companies. Don't miss the chemist by the White Horse which has a glorious 'museum piece' window display from an earlier age.

Even the street itself is worth noting. As the High Street loops over a rise into The Quadrant you will see where the horses dug their heels in to haul loads up the gradient and

View of Dorking

cut away the road surface so that it is now far lower than the pavement. That has had to be walled up in a most attractive way and shoppers are protected from plunging over by cast iron posts and rails. This all makes a subtle but significant contribution to the townscaping and fortunately the iron work is preserved. So are the stone sets that cobble the street edges down by the White Horse – another nice detail, also found at Farnham, and a smart reminder underfoot to explorers that are about to walk out into the traffic!

If you are trying to cross the road at The Quadrant there is another nice detail that is easy to miss – the water pump, with its top extended up into a cast iron sign board. The lettering of 'Guildford' has had to be whitened over in case it diverts traffic down a one-way street.

Leading off from here is South Street, and almost immediately a glance to the left will reward you with another of Dorking's attractive little peeps – an ornamental archway.

The house beyond has a rustic porch etc in 'Cottage ornée' style while the house before it stands proud and firm in its classical style.

Further up, Butter Hill takes you even higher (wheelchair users take note) with views across the town to the spire of St Martin's and the downs beyond. The Friends Meeting House stands here. It is not very old (1846) but replaces an earlier one of 1709 in West Street. Dorking's connections with the Quakers go right back to the time of George Fox, their founder in the mid 17th century. Anyone interested in this topic will find the lives of the local Patching family of interest.

Other Nonconformists were gathering here in their early days too: Congregationalists in 1662, and then Wesley came in 1764 followed by another nine visits, resulting in a Methodist chapel being started in South Street. It is also the Nonconformists who have contributed the most dignified corner to the street scenes with their United Reformed church in West Street. Its regular classical dignity, set back behind a quadrangle of lawn, calmly invites a closer approach to God's ministry – very different from the passion of the evangelists who once had to work so hard in this district.

THE MILL POND AND PARISH CHURCH

Little footways and narrow streets catch the medieval spirit of the town as they bring you from the central area down to this lower level. This is also thought to be the site of the Roman settlement but little is understood of Roman Dorking. Tantalising fragments of evidence are dug up periodically and the archaeologists try to check all development sites, but early Dorking is proving elusive and secretive. Indeed there is surprisingly little of great interest in the town to represent any of its past days.

The mint garden was certainly something different, but survives only as an intriguing street name in the attractive district west of the church. There was a small distillery to the west of the town, at Milton Street, which began about 1895 and lasted about 20 years. It encouraged the local growing of the herb and at one time fields of it stretched up the side of the downs. Another mint centre was at Banstead, while

Leatherhead distilled lavender as did West Byfleet which also produced rose water.

Of the old church nothing remains except some monuments banished up the tower. These include one to Abraham Tucker, philosopher, writer, land improver, and the man who helped finance an early scheme to provide a better water supply to the town. Alas the wooden pipes burst.

In the churchyard is buried the playwright and translator of Italian, John Hoole, who unfortunately died on a visit to Dorking in 1803. Indeed, the district has attracted dozens of well known or interesting people, 80 or more, depending how strong a connection you allow. The Lords of the Manor, for example, include families of national importance – de Warenne, de Clare, Howard, Mowbray, Stanley, Arundel. The best known resident is from our own times, the composer and conductor Ralph Vaughan Williams, who contributed as much to the life of the district as he did to British music. So often these two interests overlapped, as with his long involvement with the Leith Hill Music Festival which he conducted from 1905 right up until 1953. St Martin's church and the church room were regular settings for his activities, captured in delightful quick sketches by Denis Harvey, showing the familiar broad shoulders of Vaughan Williams bent over his music before the great cross of St Martin's during rehearsals for the *St John Passion*.

Not only can we enjoy the music associated with this setting, but still walk the narrow streets through the irregular old buildings by the church that Vaughan Williams enjoyed, and know that parts of the surrounding countryside are preserved for public enjoyment through his efforts. His house is owned by The National Trust, although not open to the public. Parts of the grounds have public access and are especially worth visiting in May for the glory of the rhododendrons.

From the church there are paths down to the Pipp brook which was the life force of early Dorking, providing water and power. The most attractive reminder of these days is the great mill pond that lies in the dip down here. Beset with mallard, coot and moorhen, edged with trees and backed by grassland, it is just the place to rest after walking the town.

Egham

If I had the time to study a small Surrey town in detail it would be Egham. It offers such a variety of themes from its past. Back in medieval times it was a holding of Chertsey Abbey and a centre of discontent, rising against the abbey with Thorpe and Chobham in 1369. The Court Rolls were burned. In 1381 Egham joined in with the Peasants' Revolt. Magna Carta was of course sealed here in 1215. From Tudor times come reminders of its place in the Royal Forest of Windsor, with a hunting lodge that has developed into Great Fosters Hotel. There we can enter beneath the arms of Elizabeth I and see Anne Boleyn's room (guide book available at hotel). Egham was also a coaching stop on the Great Bath Road and for hundreds of years had busy wharves on the Thames. The railways had their effect, too, of course. Out by the river is the former centre of horse racing, the Magna Carta site, the J F Kennedy memorial and the Royal Air Force memorial.

Despite all this Egham is a demure little town. It has been described as 'characterless' by Sir Nikolaus Pevsner, by which I suppose he meant there is no harmony or continuity. That was 25 years ago and nothing has changed that situation. It does, however, turn those deficits into a virtue – the amazing shambles of discontinuity welded together by the winding street creates a variety that is hard to beat in Surrey. There is nothing worth looking at except the total.

Starting at the west end of the High Street, Strodes is likely to catch the eye. Now a sixth form college, it was originally founded by Henry Strode in 1704. The building we see today dates only from 1915, reviving an early style of brickwork but without the verve. Almost opposite is a small public garden with a large water pump placed rather incongruously in the centre. It is a good piece of early 19th century work removed here for safe keeping from the Glanty – the north-east side of the town where the old main road ran through (now the A30). The pump was used to raise water for laying the dust on the road, hence its large size.

18 Miles from Hyde Park Corner

19th century water pump and 18th century milestone at Egham

Moving east we come to the mock Jacobean Barclays Bank, noticeable for being white. Inscribed Ashby and Co, established 1796, rebuilt 1896, it is the one building of character in the street. It is best seen from Station Road opposite and as you approach it from down there you can see at once the importance it plays as a focal point in the townscape at this junction. Notice too the fine iron gate before the door.

The National Westminster Bank a little further east shows how a very large modern red brick building can be successful in an old street. It follows the building line and in scale happens to be correct because it pairs up well with its neighbours, especially the Literary Institute (a museum). The Institute is 18th century and more intent upon its self-importance than being attractive. Originally it must have been very imposing when there were no other two-storey buildings to rival it.

Then comes the oldest survivor of the coaching days, The Red Lion. The inscription says 1521, but what we see is a 17th century tile-hung exterior. Unlike so many of this date in Surrey, the brick and tile is very dark, looking gloomy in dull weather. (The atmosphere inside was far more cheery!)

Now for a smile. Look on the same side for R Clarke's the butcher's. Viewed from the other side of the street we see it is of long standing – established 1877, when butchers raised their own meat, hence 'Butcher and Grazier'. But look each side. A pair of beautiful coloured and glazed cattle heads proudly gaze outwards; lovely pieces of Art Deco.

Church Road curves into High Street as it might in any town but with the church and war memorial on the corner there might well have been scope for more attractive town-scaping. As it is, the church is hidden behind yew trees and that is the best place for it. Back in 1817-20 Henry Rhodes took the ideas of Sir John Soane and tried to give the village a dash of neoclassicism. Instead, they got a heavy dollop of dreariness. The best is the oval cupola-like tower when seen catching the sun above the trees by travellers on the M25.

What is worth seeing is the lych gate, put in its present position in 1938, having formerly been the wooden porch of the old church. Only a few carved examples remain in Surrey. The predominant decoration of this one is the moulding but the front elevation has its spandrels pierced with quatrefoils and daggers. The sides are each pierced with a trefoil-headed light. It is good quality work of the 15th century. Also unusual for Surrey is the large collection of carved headstones in the dreary churchyard beyond. Most appear to have come from the same workshop. There is also more than the usual number of table tombs but mostly plain or weathered unreadable. John Wesley 'passed this way and preached' in 1744.

A detour up Hummer Road from this junction brings you to the shop of J Stopps and Son. They were established in 1898 and have a superb Victorian corner shop. It is red brick with a slate roof, very simple and very effective – a perfect example.

Looking over the car park almost opposite, you can see Egham has preserved an example of the malt houses once so common. It is another fine piece of Victoriana and all the better for being complete with its white cowl.

Further along the High Street we find evidence of the infant town developing a new urban status in the 1920s. First comes the Egham Urban Council fire station of 1928, quite in keeping, and then across the sharp bend in the High Street, the police station. How domestic it looks and indeed today it does provide police accommodation but those same left-hand rooms were originally the CID offices. It is a far cry from the daunting bureaucratic blocks built for our police today.

Lastly, over the road and round the corner is a milestone built into number 109. Not many survive and this is an 18th century one: 18 miles from Hyde Park Corner.

Away to the north-east is a second nucleus worth visiting and that is The Hythe. It is by the end of Staines Bridge so all the main roads lead there. It is easier and safer to enter by the first turning left off Chertsey Lane to the east of the bridge.

EGHAM HYTHE

To see Anne Boleyn, a jolly farmer and a swan all at the same time you need simply to visit Egham Hythe where these three pubs keep the old waterfront alive. The Hythe was the harbour for Staines and lies on the Surrey bank of the Thames opposite the market square. Between them, former bridges spanned the river but the current Staines Bridge is a little way upstream at the west end of the Hythe.

From it you look down on this ancient little thoroughfare and approach it down beside a lengthy terrace of old cottages, white at either end and tile-hung in the central section (lovely big rough tiles). They set the tone for the nucleus of 17th and 18th century buildings that make up the Hythe. It is quite a surprise to find such a corner when the approaches are wide busy roads through modern development.

Although old, these are only the latest buildings. It has been a vital place since life began around here. There have recently been excavations of the nearby prehistoric settlement; Staines Museum has an impressive model of the

Roman town. But it is as a bridge point that this spot has been significant for so long. The Romans built one; their name for Staines was Ad Pontes which means 'the bridges'. In early medieval times Staines Bridge was the only bridge west of London so when the latter was in rebel hands Staines was strategically vital. The Hythe has certainly seen some comings and goings. (The present bridge is noted in the entry for Staines.)

Waterfronts are always cramped places and this is no exception. Consequently building plots have to be constantly re-used so, although the oldest buildings we see look 17th and 18th century, they have all their predecessors beneath them. The Swan Hotel looks 18th century but incorporates older work. (Samuel Pepys was a regular visitor.) The Jolly Farmer looks the same but parts of that are at least a century earlier. The former has the nicety of a white stucco finish whereas the latter, and The Boleyn, are left in plain red brick. The Boleyn was a private house long before it was a hotel. It all harmonises well – Surrey's finest waterfront.

A white post stands in the triangle of grass at the top of the Hythe by the bridge. It is a London Corporation boundary post (see the city's heraldry on it), sometimes called a coal tax post. Several hundred were set up following the Coal and Wine Duties Continuance Act of 1861 on all routes, whether by road, rail or water, into the area administered by the Corporation of London. Any coal passing these points was taxed. Originally the coal tax was to raise funds for rebuilding London after the Great Fire of 1666 but by the 19th century the Continuation Acts directed the funds to be spent within the area for public benefit. Through this system it was possible to cease charging tolls on Staines Bridge in 1871 – a very popular decision locally! This tax system ceased in 1890. Coal traffic on the river ceased in the 1930s.

Next to this post is a roundabout but it was nearly chosen as the site for one of the railway stations. The factory site beyond saw the building of Lagonda cars and later Petters' engines. It is a far cry from when William Carpenter came home from a day at his coachbuilding premises in Staines High Street, home to Hythe End House, next to The Cottage which has been converted from his own coach-house. Some

80 or more coaches a day passed this way so Mr Carpenter was kept busy. He was described in the 1878 Post Office Directory as 'Coachbuilder of note' and he was too, serving the Khedive of Egypt, Prince Christian, the Prince of Wales, and Queen Victoria. This was not a favoured route of Queen Victoria though. She asked to by-pass Staines because she didn't like its smell!

Epsom

Belgium has not contributed much to Surrey but here it does in name. Spa is a town south-east of Liege where medicinal waters were exploited from 1326. By the 16th century there were spas all over Europe. The first in England to have permanent buildings was here in Epsom, after the mineral waters were discovered in 1618.

Epsom became Europe's foremost spa but you would never guess that today as the A24 drops you gently off the downs into the west end of the High Street. It was at this junction that a new well and all its social life developed but there is little left to excite the casual visitor today.

Look around and you won't find another Bath or Cheltenham. You will find a high street wide enough for a market (founded 1685) and it is a long high street, too, but the view is blocked by a 'grotesque' clock tower of 1847-1848. It might offend the art critics but I like it simply because it is the only bit of Epsom that is self-assertive.

The small village of Epsom blossomed brilliantly and early, only to be frosted in 1753 by Sir Richard Russell's promotion of an alternative health cure – bathing in the sea. Epsom was kept so busy with the crowds, from Queen Anne and Prince George of Denmark down to 'the impertinent ill-bred city wives', that it never had time to make permanent its own importance. When Pepys came there was no accommodation available. By the time George III and Queen Charlotte came there was no need – they didn't take the waters. Times had changed for Epsom and again since then. It is ironic that its most assertive building should be a clock!

The fame of 'Epsom Salts' has lived on, of course. Older readers at least will perhaps remember the purgative powers of even a small amount in a glass of water ! Shudder then at the thought of taking three pints on three consecutive days! That is what 'taking the waters' involved. They couldn't take it though; they dropped with exhaustion from the purging and the vomiting. How desperate they must have been to cure their ills. It is even sadder that so many people suffered this under social pressure to be part of the current fashion of society. Nowadays we happily dose plants with it instead, to cure their magnesium deficiency.

HIGH STREET TO CHURCH STREET
The High Street is, in design, a fine piece of townscape, the usual Surrey market place as a long narrow triangle, walled in with buildings. At the narrow end is a crossroads and then the line continues as Upper High Street. Just to confuse you, this is downhill of the High Street! Just to spoil your ease of exploring, it is also the main A24 and can become severely congested with traffic, so choose your time carefully.

At any time the High Streets are spoiled by their buildings. About ten in the High Street proper saw the glory of Epsom in its spa days but these are not especially eye-catching. (But see Church Street). Instead there is such an awful disarray of works from the 19th and 20th centuries that it needs to be seen. It shows so well just how good is West Street in Farnham, another long busy shopping street but where regard for scale, proportion, roof lines etc produces something of national importance. In Epsom all the variety disintegrates into distraction. Only the long line of the overall design strings it together. It is particularly noticeable at the eastern end where it branches into three. The junction was rebuilt with some thought to creating good townscaping, by curving the buildings round the corners. It is a big space, accepting large-scale frontages, which, in their soft coloured brick, could look impressive. Instead they are overpowered by their neighbouring mish-mash and by their own streetline of little multi-coloured shop fronts.

Round the corner into East Street is one of the town's conservation areas, Prospect Place, 'which reflects in its form the double and single strips of the former Great North Field of Epsom enclosed in about 1869'.

CHURCH STREET
The walk up to the parish church becomes all the more rewarding after a look at the High Street. Here you will find the finer Georgian Houses to remind us of the days when Epsom was viewed with esteem as a select place to reside.

First though, a modern building is likely to catch the eye – The United Reformed church. Success stories from the Nonconformists abound in Surrey but Epsom had to wait so long to join the list. High society that came to Epsom brought largely an adherence to the established order and that meant the Church of England. Their servants were expected to conform too. Epsom doesn't break the usual pattern with any story of a grand beginning. The first Nonconformist meeting is often quoted as 1688 but that hides the truth. That was the year that James I issued what has become known as the Toleration Act, making such meetings legal, but it didn't of course produce Nonconformists overnight. They already existed, meeting in secret, ever fearful of discovery, persecution and imprisonment. The farms in the Epsom downland certainly had a secret life of their own.

Even so, official meetings in town did not flourish as they did in places like Guildford and Godalming. Even after a hundred years they were still struggling, relying upon a few 'persons of opulence and their families', until the chapel was forced to close. It remained so for over 20 years and was then revived but again, not without difficulties. Now they have a very distinctive modern church.

Next door is a very pleasing group of Numbers 45 and 47 of the 17th and 18th centuries. Notice the different designs as reflected in their chimney positions, one central the other at gable ends. More and more houses were being built on this town fringe, like the one next door and Number 12 opposite, all rather close to the grandest, The Cedars (now Social Services offices). Nine bays of red and yellow brick with a raised centre and raised corners to the parapet all give this an impressive appearance. It is early Georgian, probably from the end of the 17th century and the freshness of the style to the designer shows. No stereotyped doorway here. This one greets its callers with a bold, dark coat of arms. Similarly, Richmond House, just up the road, invites thoughts of carriages sweeping up to its long front. Unfortunately it is rather close to the road for that to have been done with much panache.

This, you will see was a regular problem here where land for development was obviously limited. Not only are the houses close together but some, like 59A (Stone House, 18th century), were built right on the roadside. Notice how this one was extended in the 19th century (now Number 59) to make a good bold block.

There were houses with more expansive grounds, set further back, but their pattern has been disguised by modern infilling. The preserved garden walls give a good visual clue to the explorer on site. Others have become public open spaces, like Ashley Park. Additional interest is provided by the number of stables, coach-houses etc that have been converted into modern homes.

Up Church Street attention is now diverted from Georgian architecture by Ye Olde Kings Head with a contrasting pub-style front. Even this building dates back to the 18th century though. Opposite is a small church square, just like a Thames-side village such as Shepperton or Thorpe. To the left is the great hulk of Church House with lovely textured brick from the 18th century but with very odd proportions in the fenestration. That's nothing. Look at the west front of the church.

THE PARISH CHURCH

Epsom did not fall back into obscurity when the mineral waters went out of fashion. It remained a popular place for summer visits, especially after Westminster Bridge was completed in 1750 and encouraged Londoners to explore Surrey. By this time horse-racing on Epsom Downs was becoming very attractive; the annual Derby was founded in 1780.

Epsom's old village church was a very poor thing for a place of such social importance. However, the congregations fluctuated seasonally, making it more difficult to raise funds for improvement, until 1818 when the Church Building Act was passed, to increase church accommodation. This was intended for London, but the Commissioners allocated money for the building of a new church at Addlestone and for Epsom they agreed to fund a new façade in flint and stucco, in 1824. The Commissioners were not expected to allocate more of the Government fund than was necessary and the west front of Epsom church shows that they did not.

The Derby Arms on Epsom Downs

Inside it is very different. It is full of light. The nave roof has been lifted high and so have the arcades on their slim piers, all allowing maximum light from the large aisle windows of clear glass. It has all been redecorated in recent years and the blue vaults of the aisles add to the daylight effect. The nave roof has been painted deep yellow and the beams chocolate brown. Decide for yourselves what you make of that!

In 1907 fresh work was begun at the east end and, as it was entrusted to Sir Charles Nicholson, it is of quality. Nevertheless, it is difficult to see what he was trying to do until one knows of the plans to raise the church to cathedral status. Then we see he created a central crossing and planned side transepts to develop a strong cruciform design, all of which came to nothing. Poor old Epsom; nothing seems to go right for long!

The east end of the church attracts you through a fine modern open screen, to view the equally fine east window. It is a figurative design in coloured glass set into clear glass – dramatic. A couple of memorials to its left are of interest. There is a plaque (one of three here by Flaxman) to the Rev John Parkhurst whose work included two Bible lexicons. Below that is the memorial to the Rev Jonathan Boucher with an intriguing inscription telling us 'his loyalty to his king remained unshaken even when the madness of the people raged furiously against him; and for his conscience sake he resigned ease and affluence in America to endure hardship and poverty in his native land but the Lord gave him twice as much as before.' It is a story from the American War of Independence when Boucher was a friend of George Washington but found himself unable to support the colonists' cause. He preached against it with such danger to his life that he resorted to taking pistols with him into the pulpit. That is when he realised it was time to flee.

Two other items are worth a look before leaving. Down by the west door is displayed a 'vinegar Bible' wherein the printer rendered vinyard as vinegar in the Parable of the Vineyard. Then over the door are the royal arms of the Hanoverian period; not rare but always posing the problem of how to incorporate the complicated German heraldry into our own. Here is a common solution, to superimpose the Hanoverian arms in the centre of our own.

CHALK LANE AND DURDANS

If you want to see fine buildings in greater peace then follow South Street out of the central crossroads, up its continuation as Woodcote Road, until Chalk Lane branches off to the left. This is now a Conservation Area. A couple of buildings date from the 17th century, ten or so from the 18th century and there are some pleasing later ones too. Chief of all is The Durdans.

Begun in 1764 and much added to in the 19th century, it was the home of the 5th Earl of Rosebery, the firm Liberal imperialist who succeeded Gladstone as Prime Minister in March 1894. He failed to get his Liberal legislation through the House of Lords and resigned in the June of the next year.

He gave up the Liberal leadership the following year and turned to racing. As a racehorse owner he found success and four horse tombs are now preserved monuments at Durdans.

He himself is commemorated by Rosebery Park behind the High Street. A couple of political successes have persisted too. The Scottish Office was largely his creation from when he was Lord Privy Seal, having been responsible previously for Scottish Affairs when under-secretary at the Home Office. Less popular was the introduction of Death Duties in the 1894 Budget, the only successful budget of his short premiership, before Cabinet disharmony forced his resignation. He was better with horses and had many years left to enjoy them, not dying until 1929, aged 72.

Horses still attract thousands to keep up the old traditions of a visit to Epsom in the first week of June – Derby Week. Don't come to explore the town then!

On the other hand, it is the best time to experience something special. There is nothing quite like the British out en masse to enjoy themselves. A great crescent of the Downs is suddenly encrusted with vehicles, overtopped by the fun fair, drenched with smells from the hot food vans and swilling with people – not just the horse fraternity but fair folk and 'travellers', ladies and gentlemen and all those pretending to be, and no one caring when they forget. It is all the fun of Derby week. To enjoy it you don't have to love horse racing, just to love people.

Just as suddenly it is all over. The Downs are bare again, save for the lines of workmen clearing tons of litter and how speedily they do it too. Quiet returns and the gentler flow of regular visitors to enjoy the views over to London, the wide spaces and the wind in their faces or under their kites, rich with the scent of wild mignonette and the calls of passing meadow pipits.

Esher

Esher has a more formal dignity than most of its neighbours and retains its Georgian style centre. That's quite remarkable considering the traffic congestion it caused before the by-pass was built. Other authorities might well have bulldozed straight through.

Esher centre is still a very busy place – probably too much so for the people who work and shop here but for the casual visitor with time to spare the traffic edging round the central green all helps to keep the place alive. Towns have always developed as service points for travellers, both long-distance on the roads or short-distance from the neighbouring countryside. Modern traffic-free centres are changing that role.

Here the traditions continue. Two large bears survey the scene from the roof of The Bear Inn, reminding us that Esher was an important stop on a coaching route. Before that the bishops of Winchester had one of their country estates here; a convenient stopping place en route between Winchester and London.

Esher's other great estate was Claremont, the grounds of which have been restored by The National Trust as England's earliest surviving landscape garden. The house was made famous when used by Queen Victoria and her family but that's well documented elsewhere. There's a reminder though on the town centre green in the form of a cast iron water pump presented to the parish by Victoria.

The old parish church of St George is also famous and well documented for it's one of the very few built in Tudor times. Indeed it's sometimes described as England's first Protestant church but it's easy to pick holes in that claim. The interior is largely as the Georgians left it and so it's now preserved as an ancient monument, open Saturday afternoons.

Christ Church serves instead today. Shamefully, it's largely ignored by the guide books yet it is one of the county's finest Victorian town churches, built in 1853 by Benjamin Ferrey.

He was an architect with a sense of place. His building of

St George's church, Esher

the church beside the green at Brockham created something of great landscape value and still very popular with photographers today. Here at Esher he did the same, putting a fine building on a rise overlooking The Green and with a spire that signals the location of Esher for miles around. At Brockham his interior is stark and boring but here we step into a church that fulfils expectations.

There was more money available for one thing, due to the royal connections. Victoria's uncle, Leopold of Saxe-Coburg, gave £1,000 to it. He married Princess Charlotte, only daughter of George IV and heir to the throne, in 1816 and it was for them that Claremont was bought. Sadly this very popular lady was so soon to die in childbirth, in November, 1817, aged 21. Her monument is in St George's.

Leopold was called to the Belgian throne in 1831 but he wasn't forgotten. Queen Victoria remembered this was the uncle she sat next to as a girl during church services in St George's. She had him commemorated in 1867 by Susan Durant with a fine marble effigy, lying on a couch wearing the insignia of the Order of the Golden Fleece. That was transferred here from Windsor and is 'hidden' in the choir vestry.

Victoria's last visit to St George's was in 1847, for the next year Claremont became the home of the exiled French royal family, until 1866. Then it was used by another Prince Leopold – her son, the Duke of Albany, and his wife. Whenever Victoria was staying with them at Claremont this was the church she attended. When he died in 1884 he was commemorated here with a fine bust by the local sculptor, F. Williamson. It wasn't his only royal subject. He carved a fine profile of the Queen herself on the occasion of her jubilee, to be seen in Mickleham church. His carving is also to be seen in Christ Church on his own monument.

Before leaving Christ Church there's one other monument to see – that of Sir Richard Drake (1603) kneeling up on the south wall but originally in St George's. To this man, at Esher, were sent the prisoners of war from the defeat of the Spanish Armada. It's presumed he was a kinsman of Sir Francis Drake but recent research has failed to trace the family connection. Nevertheless, it was with great glee that Sir Francis sent the prisoners back, especially Don Pedro de Valdes. 'Their Don Pedro is a man of great estimation with the King of Spain, and thought next in his army to the Duke of Sidonia,' he wrote to Queen's Secretary, Walsingham, requesting his prisoners be delivered up to the Queen personally. The commemorated Sir Richard was the man who took charge of them.

That all seems a long time ago when you leave Christ Church and step back into the attractively suburbanised scene outside. The Green is several greens, mown like lawns, with mature trees around and smart houses, all creating fine townscaping. Over the back is the development of Esher Place, used by the bishops of Winchester and also lived in by the notorious Cardinal Wolsey. Of the early house, built about 1460, only the gatehouse remains, altered by William Kent about 1730. It's known as Waynflete's Tower after the bishop who had it built.

More interesting is that we know who actually built it – a mason named John Cowper. He probably belonged to a family of masons, as two or three are recorded working on Winchester College. This John then went on to work on Eton College until the downfall of its patron, Henry VI, following the Battle of Northampton. Then this great craftsman seems to have been taken on by Bishop Waynflete himself, for he's recorded working on some of the Bishop's major enterprises, such as the church of Tattershall in Lincolnshire and the school at Wainfleet itself. Esher Place was one of the major enterprises. It's so important because John Cowper transferred his skills with stone to promoting a relatively new material – bricks.

Behind Esher Place runs the river Mole and by the bridge is Waylands Farm, once leased by a certain William Duckitt. He's now forgotten but was once so famed as an agricultural pioneer and inventor of farm machinery that he attracted a visit from George III – Farmer George. The two became friends. Many other nobles came to Waylands, all intent upon learning new methods of agricultural improvement. It didn't stop here. The Duckitt tombstone in St George's churchyard (east side, table tomb) records the son dying at the Cape of Good Hope, 'to which settlement he was sent with a large establishment by His Majesty Geo 3rd to introduce his father's system and implements of agriculture into that colony in the year 1800.'

The Duckitt lands have survived modern development and retain links with old traditions. The farm is now a riding centre and other land became Sandown Race Course. Despite first appearances there's an enormous wealth of heritage at Esher.

Farnham

More variety! This time you will find a 'planned town'; not a modern railway centre but something much rarer, an early medieval one. Recent archaeological work (1986) suggests that it was planned earlier than previously thought, that it is the work of Henry de Blois, Bishop of Winchester, from the 1130s when he had the town ditch dug and the street laid out with burgage plots, on the southern slope of the hill between his castle at the top and the river Wey at the bottom.

The best approach is by the A287 from the north which brings you to the castle and then spirals down round its hill to burst out of the trees at the head of Castle Street. It is arguably Surrey's finest street scene. From this high point it drops and broadens into a long triangular market place, bordered each side with Georgian architecture and concluding with the cross-street of The Borough. Beyond lies the parish church and the water meadows before the land rises again beyond the river, all the way to Hindhead.

This, some have claimed, is England's finest Georgian town, prompting others to deny it loudly. Certainly it is not another Bath. What you will find is each neighbour trying to make their house different from the next but all in the same style, so there is infinite variety in doorways and windows, cornices and parapets, stucco and brick and in the way the very bricks are bonded together. The houses don't make a great sweep of a scene either but retain their individuality. This arose partly by accident, for once there were spaces between them. Then, as the owners prospered in this thriving market town, so they needed extra servants' quarters which they created by extending over the gap. That is why each joins the other at a slight angle and why there is no monotony in the roof line and why these infills are of a slightly later date than their parent house. Some kept the gaps as carriage entrances and just bridged over the top but these have mostly been blocked today.

Some of the variety was dictated by law not fashion. The various Fire Acts at the beginning of the 18th century

Farnham castle

banished wooden cornices and promoted parapets, condemned windows flush with the wall and caused them to be set back. All this story is told by the buildings of Farnham. Do choose a quiet time to wander and to stop and stare. There is nothing quite as fine as summer evening light falling on Farnham brick.

CASTLE STREET

Depending where you park the car, the first thing you are likely to notice is that the sides of the market place are cobbled. It is not a good idea to be overheard calling them cobbles in Surrey though! They are 'sets' – little lumps of local ironstone. In sunlight after rain they glow richly in pinks and plums and reflected sky blue.

Let's now look at a selection of the buildings that make

Farnham so highly esteemed. Walking up the right-hand side, Numbers 74/76 are still attractive at street level, with two styles of bow window and a flat shell-decorated doorway. Then Number 70 shows the Fire Act transition, with a parapet to shield the roof timbers but with windows still kept flush with the brickwork. They still have their internal wooden shutters. With Number 68 we are back to the vernacular with a sample of tile-hanging, which, due to all the surrounding variety, does not look out of place.

Each building attracts our attention in different ways. At Number 68 it is that special orange colour of local Farnham brick. At Number 63 it is the bow-headed windows, another way of reducing the risk of falling woodwork in a fire. Numbers 61 and 62 reward comparison from the different ways their bricks have been bonded to all their individuality, from recessed windows to projecting door bay, to the segmental arcading of the ground floor – three bays here but five above. Number 62 was built first in a rather standard copybook style whereas its neighbour has individual flair.

Now we have to change our thinking. The almshouses are not Georgian at all. A gable stone informs us, 'These almshouses were erected by Andrew Windsor Esq. in 1619 for the Habitation and Relief of Eight poor honest and Impotent Persons.' They are not rated as great architecture but surely they are a great exercise in the picturesque and should not be altered. Indeed, from the adjoining Park Row we can see how modern extensions have been added to the rear. Who wants to look at that though, when you're in the most attractive of the Georgian side streets? From it you can reach the extensive grassiness of the Park for a rest or climb to a higher level to survey the town, (stiled entrance unsuitable for wheelchairs).

Back in Castle Street we have reached a reminder that this part was the ancient medieval town and Numbers 45/46 are timber framed buildings. Their Georgianised brick fronts should not fool anyone for long because the proportions are those of an older age. Here too the old building plots remain, with front gardens thrusting out to close the main part of the street. The castle at the top is open several days a week but it is a very steep walk with many steps so explorers may prefer to retrace their steps to their car and drive up. Walk down the other side of the street where there is another fine sequence of buildings.

It would be tedious to enthuse further on the variety here too but don't miss the grand 18th century house that has the distinction of being set back beyond a front garden, has gate piers and cast iron overthrow. If you can manage to hear the jingle of carriage harness or picture a lady's long rich fabrics in the evening light then Farnham is really getting to you!

THE GRANGE

Often listed in Castle Street is The Grange, one of only four really fine Queen Anne houses in the county. It is not in the main street though. As you drive up to the castle so you will find Old Park Lane branches off to the left and in that junction stands the house. You can glimpse it from the road without invading their privacy, and spot the architect's nightmare of having two floors on one face but three on the adjoining face. They are of different dates: the oldest still has lead casement windows while the latest has Queen Anne sash windows. It is usually dated 1700-1710 and said to be one of the finest in the whole country. Locally its nearest rival is Willmer House in West Street. That you can go and see, inside and out, without annoying anyone because it is the town museum.

WEST STREET

Charles I on his way to execution was held prisoner for one night in Vernon House (now the public library) and so this is the house that is most likely to be pointed out to visitors. Others are more worthy of a close look but first there is an ordinary-looking 19th century workshop to see, out at the far western end.

The plaque on the wall informs us 'John Henry Knight's car, one of Britain's earliest petrol driven vehicles, was built here by George Parfitt at the Elliott Reliance Works 1895.' That gives enthusiasts enough information to follow up the story and fit it with other centres of early car manufacture in Surrey, at Guildford, Hersham, Staines and Woking. Here, further information is available at the museum.

Vernon House, West Street, Farnham.
A. Hawkins. 1985.

Vernon House in West Street, Farnham

Now for the prime buildings. Bethune House, basically Doric, shows the Palladian style at its best, having no doubt been designed from mid 18th century copybook plates. It is not entirely stereotyped though. The doorway, looking familiar enough, is notably rich; the window proportions vary from floor to floor and so do the glass panes; to maintain balance two of the upper windows are 'blind' – glass over the brick wall.

Willmer House comes next, with a flourish of Baroque of national importance. Here we can see inside for it is the museum (wheelchair access to ground floor displays at the side). Here, too, we can catch up on local worthies such as the politician and outspoken writer William Cobbett, born and buried in Farnham, or Stephen Elmer ARA, said to be England's finest painter of the still life with dead game. His home is now 33/33A in this long and varied street.

The street is so varied that the eye even accepts the former grammar school building in its non-Georgian style. It has the architectural manners not to ruin the roof line nor to present anything but wide flat surfaces to the street. Break those up and you get something as hideously out of keeping as the post office over the road. Further along, when West Street becomes The Borough, there is the Spinning Wheel – a half-timbered building with richer than usual patterning. It looks a mock effort but most of it is original – just over-restored. Again it manages to fit in, providing an accent of contrast at the foot of Castle Street where it is acceptable. The National Westminster Bank on the other hand, although having earned praise, seems to me to exert its own self importance a little too assuredly. Its proportions are too expansive, it is too high and too lavish – just look at that cornice! Yes, it is Victorian, 1860, when the good manners of the Georgian Age had lost their tongue.

DOWNING STREET AND CHURCH LANES
A familiar street name and, at this stage of a walk round Farnham, some familiar Georgian scenery too. It all reflects the prosperity of the town, from what was boldly hailed as the largest corn market outside London and, when that declined, from the wealth of the very extensive hop 'grounds'. (They are not 'gardens' here; that is the word from Kent).

Downing Street drops down to a sharp left bend which presumably marks the expected upper limit of any flooding in the water meadows that fringed the river Wey beyond. The eye is carried round that bend by two of the more important houses. Number 3 has a renowned cornice and doorway of 1717 – a presentment of Baroque to vie with Willmer House. Note how the doorway is actually carved out of bricks.

Enough of the Georgians. Your eye will be caught by Lower Church Lane running off the corner towards the church. It is close, dignified and surfaced with ironstone sets (wheelchair users take note). It is the stereotype of an 'old fashioned' street and one that carries its pleasures on into Middle Church Lane and then adds more in Upper Church Lane. Fortunately they are neither so pretty as to be sentimentalised nor so manicured as to resemble a Hollywood film set. They don't work by showing-off but by creating a distinctive sense of place and that is created not by what is there so much as the spaces between – the contrast

Moor Park Gatehouse, Farnham

between the close lanes and the open churchyard they lead to.

From top or bottom you get the artist's favourite views to the fine medieval church, well set-off in a large sloping rough grassland. Especially pictorial is the view from the bottom corner to the central tower seen between gate piers with their iron overthrow complete with lantern. St Andrew's is a big church from when Farnham's wealth was not dependent upon either hops or corn but the medieval wool trade.

Inside it is very disappointing due to an over zealous Benjamin Ferrey in 1855. If you enjoy a big empty space then that is just what he has left you. He also left two medieval wooden screens, now across the north and south chapels. As so few of the three dozen churches with surviving screens or fragments in Surrey are in town churches (the best is at Reigate) it is worth noting these.

They were never part of the same parclosed chapel as they do not match, the northern being the more delicate. It has eight lights over its doorway instead of the six used in the southern. There you will find the usual Surrey style, in four bays of two lights each, separated by muntins with simple crocketing. The small buttresses on the western side are restorations, as is the small basal kerb. The mullions between the lights in each bay have been renewed also, and not quite to the usual style so they may not be replicas of the originals. Similarly, the scarring elsewhere reveals that the finials etc are not as originally conceived. Nevertheless, what does remain of the original all helps to build up a picture of pre-Reformation craftsmanship and fashion in Surrey churches.

Fashion and craftsmanship, that is really what Farnham shows better than other places in Surrey. For something completely different you can join the end of the North Downs Way and walk over heathland and downland to Guildford and beyond.

Godalming

Godalming, sliding down the hillsides into the valleys of the Wey and the Ock, has been a town for over a thousand years. The church still has Anglo-Saxon work in parts. All around is a wide range of delights, some well known, like the High Street and Church Street, others less well known like Mill Lane, but in which ever direction you set off you'll find things to catch your.eye. That is what is so exciting about the town.

The itineraries chosen all begin at the railway station. A car parking space may sometimes be found in Station Road or in the station forecourt approach, at off-peak periods. The first route, along Mill Lane, is for walkers.

The old parts of adjoining Farncombe were published in *Hidden Surrey*.

MILL LANE

There are many English towns where we can still explore the narrow confines of close medieval streets but not in Surrey. Godalming provides the county's best example in the area beside the little river Ock. Through this runs Mill Lane, dropping steeply to cross the river and rising just as steeply beyond, and all with great charm.

Railway stations rarely have much to offer the non-specialist but this one should please anyone with an eye for a good period piece and it does have a more interesting story than many.

It is built of local stone which glows warm and golden in low sunshine so that is the time to try and see it. You'll find a small, homely building of 1859; in other words, before a 'railway style' was developed. When the Victorians wanted to be monumental they certainly could, but their other great skill was in responding to human scale, whether in developing whole new villages, like Holmbury St Mary, or in single buildings like this one.

Of the same date is Haslemere station and if you can bring memories of that here you'll appreciate Godalming's all the more. Similarly, Farnham station is ten years earlier, house-like but with none of the domestic charm that you'll find here.

As for the story behind it – there was an incredible wrangle between the various railway companies. The strategic importance of a direct route between London and Portsmouth was realised at an early date but other lines came into being first, such as one to Brighton. Thus Portsmouth could be reached via Chichester but Portsmouth was such a prime objective that its station became jointly owned by three companies, with agreements over shared facilities including stretches of track.

None wanted a more direct route because the shorter distance would mean less income from fares. However, the Portsmouth Railway Company began to make positive moves which were seen as threatening by the other companies. At the other end, the London and South West Railway built a spur from Guildford to Godalming in a bid for the route. Other schemes came forward to approach Godalming from Epsom via Dorking and soon the companies were well and truly at each other's throats.

The shared track near Portsmouth was ideal for sabotage so that, even after the London and South West Railway had built the line, the first train didn't quite make it. The opposition removed the points at Portcreek Junction, blocked the route with a locomotive and removed sections of track. Thus, on December 28th 1858, the first train had to retreat back through Godalming – defeated. Due to this conflict the public on the first passenger services found themselves having to terminate at Havant and continue by bus!

This was not Godalming's first station. That was built nearer Farncombe where the spur line from Guildford had ended. Only when the Portsmouth route was finally laid was this present Godalming station built and its predecessor continued to serve Farncombe until a new station was built there in 1897. Thereafter the first Godalming station dealt only with goods and little of that remains today.

Bearing left in front of the station the road now plunges as a narrow lane to a millstream. The rapid transition is astonishing, from Victorian enterprise to that of the Middle

Ages, for this is the old town, famed for its cloth trade. It ranked with Gloucester and York, only these three places being specified in an Act of 1557.

The millstream (river Ock) cuts through in a 'villagy' sort of way with Hatch Mill beside it. It is tall and imposing nearest the road, burrowing back into the land where the water cascades down. Here we can see something more unusual. The waterwheel has been removed and a turbine installed instead. Cast clearly on the side is just what the industrial archaeologist would want to know – 'Gilbert Gilkes and Gordon Ltd. Kendal. No 4491. 1940.' The mill was built in the 18th century as a corn mill but no longer operates; there isn't even any machinery left inside. It is a Listed building, so hopefully it will continue to add distinction to this corner. Its high luccombe projecting towards the street is certainly a more impressive detail than on many Surrey watermills.

Opposite, the Old Granary complements the scene. It is just one of a whole group of half-timbered buildings in this corner that gives you the best chance in Surrey of imagining townscape of Tudor times and earlier. Tudor Cottage stands next door. How narrow is the flight of steps up the side! They really help to prod the imagination into visualising the small, close scale of the medieval town.

Among the surviving buildings are some that housed the woollen industry. The Cistercian monks introduced sheep rearing for wool into West Surrey back in the 12th century. It became secularised and continued long after the dissolution of their abbey at Waverley in 1536. One such house can now be seen by turning left into Mint Street and walking up to Number 22. Notice how the upper windows have been heightened above eaves level to allow more light to fall upon the knitting frame that was worked by the window. (Such a frame can be seen in the museum). The industry has not died out. Alan Paine Ltd still manufacture their 'fine English knitwear' entirely from natural fibres at Godalming, (Riverside) and have done so since 1907. From them came the first true cable patterned sweater. The cable stitch was reputedly invented by a local lady, Mrs Pitcher, and Pitcher, Billings and Edmunds are still trading as outfitters in the High Street.

Mint Street, Godalming

From the old weaving house, look down Station Road and the first big white house on the left hints of grander things. It is a former coach house. What a splendid central archway! Note also that the back wall is not parallel with the front. Many of the older houses are mis-shapen to fit their sites.

Next door to the coach house is another of Godalming's surprises. It was here, in 1911, that the Fudger family started the town's first cinema – note the ventilators in the roof. Evidently the building has hardly changed at all. Rivalry began in 1921 with the building of King George's Cinema in Meadrow at Farncombe. Fudger's continued until the Regal came in 1935 (see below).

Retracing your steps to the bottom end of Mint Street, the Friends Meeting House is nearly opposite. Up the steps, through the iron gate, and you'll find a simple walled garden with the suitably plain Meeting House across the top. Surrey was important in the early days of the Society of Friends. The founder, George Fox, did not neglect the county, and key supporters, like William Penn of Pennsylvania fame, were active too. It is not known when the Quakers first began meeting in Godalming but by the early 18th century they were established sufficiently to have carved 'Friends Meeting House 1714' on a board, which has survived. The present building is older but may not have been their first centre.

Continuing uphill one emerges into the main street and nearly opposite, to the right, is Stovolds Dairy Shop. It is a gem of a shop front, having a façade of blue tiles to update the older building into the Art Deco style. Before 1928 it was a butcher's shop, hence the bulls' heads on either side. That motif recurs on the butcher's in Egham High Street but there they are in natural colours whereas these are in deep blue like the rest of the work. Stovold has been a family name in west Surrey and north-east Hampshire for many generations.

Further to the right one reaches the bingo hall which was formerly the aforementioned Regal Cinema. It seems demure today but back in 1935 was quite progressive. It was the work of one of the foremost designers, Robert Cromie, whose best known work today is the Hammersmith Odeon in all its Art Deco glory. He was assisted at Godalming by the famous local architect, Sir Edwin Lutyens – at least that is what promotions claimed at the time.

Opposite is Panda House, the United Kingdom headquarters of the World Wide Fund for Nature, with further Godalming premises at Catteshall. This is one of the new style office buildings; gone the glass blocks and back to low level domesticity. Is it luck or care that produced a height and roof pitch to match the old housing immediately to its right?

Not only is the building in the latest style but so is the use of the plot. The right angle of the corner site has been ignored by placing the building diagonally across it, but as a curve to sweep the eye round. The remaining triangle has been grassed and furnished with trees. When it matures it could well make a worthwhile contribution to the townscape, depending what happens around it. At present this Ockford Road approach to the town lacks distinction. It is certainly pleasant to look across the grass to the attractive older buildings at the foot of Holloway Hill. It does seem to be part of the scene, whereas the much earlier redevelopment of Walton-on-Thames demonstrated how blocks in grassy spaces could remain nothing better than blocks in grassy spaces.

Double back past the top of Mill Lane and you'll come to the well-known junction with Church Street (which returns you to the station) and its 'Pepperpot' – the Town Hall of 1814. Note the water pump. It is large (over 2 metres) and needed to be for this was the main source of water for the town. I wonder how long the queues got? Views northwards can reveal a stone tower on top of Frith Hill built as a water tower at the turn of the century to save this problem. It blends in well because so much of it is of Bargate stone for which Godalming was the centre for its quarrying, from Romano-British times up to the Second World War. Below the tower, in Charterhouse Road the building for the pump to raise the water to the tower still survives. It is behind the Scout Hut. Further up, Charterhouse Road is spanned by an unusual bridge. The road arch is pointed Gothic, not semicircular.

Godalming's fine medieval church

WESTBROOK ROAD

Returning from the town centre down Church Street, look for Westbrook Road leading off to the right near the lowest point.

If you stop to explore the fine medieval church on your way down Church Street, then look out for the marble wall monument to Nathaniel Godbold who died in 1799. It takes us into the world of patent medicines, recording him as the 'Inventor and Proprietor of that excellent Medicine The Vegetable Balsam For the cure of Consumptions and Asthmas.' It is along the narrow leafy lane of Westbrook Road that we find his home, Westbrook House, now known as the Meath Home.

This great Georgian House was bought by Godbold in 1790 from the profits of his medicine, enabling him and his family to move here from Bloomsbury Square. They had bought more than a country house, for it also raised them into the landed gentry. They had bought a site with mills – 'a paper mill, a fulling mill, and an oil or leather mill', so they were well set to continue manufacturing. They built another mill to cash in on cotton spinning but this came to nothing. The medicines, however, continued, with daughter Louisa taking over after her father's death. Production persisted into recent times when readers may well remember the British Drug Houses operating here. (The site has now been redeveloped.)

Godbold's Vegetable Balsam was quite unusual. It contained no less than 46 herbs and fruits in four different gums 'dissolved in double distilled vinegar, with a quantity of storax dissolved in spirits of wine and oil of cinnamon', according to his patent of 1785. These were increased to 52 in the 1798 patent. There were some rather foul-tasting herbs such as wormwood, garlic and yarrow, so no doubt the inclusion of strong flavours like aniseed were most welcome! Some of the herbs, like thistles, have gone out of use but others were sound and are still in use today – yarrow, coltsfoot and angelica etc. The 13 fruits, including rose hips, would have provided good healthy doses of Vitamin C for any ailing patient! The inclusion of blackcurrants is interesting for they had been long neglected and their medicinal value only promoted in 1739.

'Godbold must have been a capitalist as well as a gentleman' commented one writer, referring to the other unusual aspect of the balsam – 'it is bottled off and kept full three years before it is fit to be administered. . .'

His work continues with the house becoming the Meath Home for asthma sufferers. In describing the house the Countess Meath draws attention to another aspect we can still enjoy today: 'Not many years ago an individual resided here who was particularly interested in tree-culture, and it is owing to his care that the grounds are so well stocked, and that trees, by no means common, are here to be admired.'

Yet another notable resident draws visitors to peep up the drive to the house. He was General James Oglethorpe, the founder of Georgia in the United States. His was an eventful and interesting life but he only gets a brief mention here as he is well documented elsewhere. As we go on up the narrow and now steep lane it must suffice to ponder upon his bringing the first American Indians to this country and putting them on public display in a pub in Godalming. Up on this hillside, too, is an old cottage called The Fort in which lived the General's sister. All the facts concerning the origin of its name are not clear today but tradition says she was a Jacobite supporter and her home was fortified when brother James refused to fight the Jacobites and fled the battlefield on the eve of Culloden. He was pursued south on charges of desertion and cowardice for which, indeed, he was found guilty. A closer look at the facts suggests more corruption than truth and the honour to his memory is well deserved.

The name of Westbrook has now been transferred to a modern house at the top of the lane, built in 1900 by the local architect H Thackeray Turner, for his own use. He made a not insignificant contribution to the county's architecture, especially when perpetuating local style and materials. He was also a lover of the beautiful county and helped preserve it, giving for example, 240 acres of Witley Common to The National Trust in 1921. His more official memorial is a pair of cottages by Eashing Bridge, which he gave to The National Trust in 1922 and have been restored in his memory. Walkers can reach Eashing from the end of this lane, otherwise turn round and retrace the route to the station.

View from the towpath along the Godalming Navigation

If it's autumn you will spot the blazing colours of a liquidambar tree in Westbrook's garden. It is most appropriate for this corner of Godalming for it was from such trees that Godbold got the storax he used in his balsam.

Godstone

Motorists beware – if you're planning to reach Godstone at Junction 7 from the anti-clockwise direction of the M25 then note that the next junction after 8 is the motorway interchange. Don't turn off yet; it'll be disastrous! Drive on and you'll reach Junction 7.

The backs of the low hills rise above the rooftops all around, for Godstone lies in a broad vale among them. There is a massive village green complete with duck pond, and dotted with horse chestnuts, candled pink and white in spring and leafed soft yellows and orange in early autumn.

Beside the Green is the little knotted village centre, unfortunately converted into a roundabout, and throttled with traffic. Defiantly it braves this and is so very attractive that visitors do too. The cottages are all huddled together with exciting little alleys between the building plots as there have been for hundreds of years. This place is really old: The Bell claims to have been founded circa 1393, The White Hart in the time of Richard II and Godstone Hotel in the 16th century and they are all grouped together.

From them a footpath takes you out past Bay Pond (a nature reserve) to the second village centre, up on the hill. Here a varied collection of old houses, a range of impressive almshouses, and the parish church make up Church Town.

BESIDE THE GREEN
Walking up the Green from the lower side there is a frieze of trees on the right, and a succession of houses in Regency White and Victorian red edge the other two sides. It is the housing along the top that lures you on.

They could so easily have been dotted Victorian villas like a row of red headstones but instead somebody went to work who had a sense of scale and place and an appreciation of contours. He worked big and bold, fitting the units close to give the impression of one range. He avoided ugliness with careful detailing and texturing. He broke the long roof line with broad gables and had carved the bargeboards on the centre and to a lesser extent a pair to the right. He allowed them to flow up the hill and to curl away from the road so that they join neatly with the end of the old village.

There the sense of the hillside continues as the pavement rises high above street level and the houses sometimes need big bold steps to their front doors. Others are nestled back, like the rosy Hare and Hounds (16th century and later) behind its chestnut tree and behind another great chestnut, the timber framing and white plaster work of another Tudor survival.

There are just so many old buildings here, in every Surrey style and material, that it's pointless to list them. Anyway, it is not their individuality that counts but their collective togetherness. Walking up into the High Street the eye is drawn to Bankside for being such a smart little 18th century house among all the rural rusticity. Why is its front face so pitted when the side isn't? Too many holes surely for nailing up roses. Perhaps they were to provide adhesion for an intended coating of stucco.

Pause by the long range (16th-19th centuries) to admire the way Thimble Cottage and its partners angle themselves round the corner. The rough-cast Malthouse Cottage is also eye-catching, dating from the early 19th century.

Down the High Street the style of the white weather-boarded house is a reminder that Kent isn't far away. It is not the Thames Valley style of north-west Surrey. Again it is the way they all flow along together that is so special here. Fortunately this centre has some two dozen houses and groups listed for protection so hopefully the ensemble won't become fragmented.

Opposite the pond at the bottom of the High Street stands the White Hart, looking like a typical example of Surrey tarting up. Look up its right-hand side though and be amazed how far back its 16th century timber framing runs; most impressive. Look up above you and read that it was founded in the reign of Richard II (the white hart was one of his personal badges). Enlarged in the reign of Elizabeth I it was 'honoured by frequent visits from her Most Gracious Majesty Queen Victoria'.

The Bell, nearly opposite, claims a near contemporary

foundation (circa 1393) although what we see is mostly from about 1700, with parts surviving from the 15th century. Then opposite is the Godstone Hotel claiming a 16th century foundation so we soon get the impression that a busy road through here is no new thing.

Don't miss the little butcher's shop here, because it still has its traditional window shutters. They open upwards and downwards rather than from each side. They are an early medieval design from when the lower one was supported horizontally to become the sales surface to the workshop within. On it could be scratched the monetary calculation tables so we still call the sales surface a 'counter'.

For a longer walk, take the footpath from here up to the church ($^1/_2$ mile perhaps) or go back to the Green area. Down the side of the pond are more attractive homes and some fine 19th century-style gardens – what people call old fashioned cottage gardens; delightful.

Part of the almshouses at Godstone

CHURCH TOWN

Celandines and bluebells, pink campion and wild parsley, drums and yellow archangels; they are all here in Church Lane, and lots more. All the old favourites from the wild flower book fill the banks to make the climb up to the church from Bullbeggars Lane all the more rewarding.

For over 300 years Surrey has provided almshouses but nowhere is there a set like these. Some are picturesque, some are imposing, some are downright utilitarian but these have combined it all since 1872. Running lengthily along the top of the bank above the lane they then turn to step carefully down to the roadside, creating a warm sunny corner through which visitors are invited to prayer in the chapel. There is no great mass of walling because the block is carefully divided up with robust timberframing in a thoroughly Tudor way, right down to the detailing of the Tudor doorways. There is no dazzling pattern of sunlit white plaster either. The infills are toned down to soft yellow ochre and any monotony there is relieved by delicate patterns of incised lines – echoes of William Morris and East Anglian pargetting. It is the work of an architect who lived locally and was one of the most esteemed in the land, Sir George Gilbert Scott. He didn't always show a sensitive hand.

He had a go at the church next door, too. It seems to have a Victorian face without a Victorian body. That's quite so. It is a medieval church that he thoroughly restored and enlarged. He made it clean-cut and smart, yet miraculously leaving it endowed with that mysterious quality of an old village church that we call feel or atmosphere. That's especially remarkable when there are so few features remaining from before his time. There is a font on which the base is square instead of octagonal like the bowl. There are the Evelyn memorials in their chapel. These include the calm white marble effigies of Sir John and his wife Dame Thomasin on their table tomb – a 17th century perpetration of medieval style (quite scarce). There is little else.

The choicest features are by Scott – the carved capitals. According to medieval symbolism the chancel arch separated the secular, earthly world of the nave from the heavenly, spiritual world of the chancel and here Scott has perpetuated that. The arch capitals are beautifully carved with the joyous angels of the heavenly host greeting us on our arrival at the gates of heaven. Across here would have stretched the chancel screen with its bressummer carved with the symbolic vine trail of life, of goodness. So it is that the first capital inside is again superbly carved with vines. Then as we move into the body of the church, so the lily symbol of the Virgin Mary is carved on the next capital. How cleverly the craftsman contrived these tall spiky emblems into a form to suit the round narrow capital and how beautiful they are too.

Finally, as we approach the communion rail, so the symbol of his crucifixion, the passion flower, decorates the nearby capital, right where the medieval Easter sepulchre would have been. Decisively the artist cut into the flowers, their stigmas representing the nails in the cross. The nearest place showing genuine medieval iconography between heaven and earth is over the West Sussex border at Hardham where the scheme of wall paintings remains very complete.

Godstone's Victorian capitals are the finest in the county. Indeed there can be few others to rival them anywhere. Go round to the north chapel and see the brambles and bracken curling round one another. Both are rare subjects; there are ferns at South Holmwood but not a patch on these. Opposite is an even rarer subject – beautifully rendered garlands of primroses. See the crinkly leaves, the heart-shaped petals and the distinct central 'eyes' – just wonderful.

Outside, the banks are full of flowers among proud spikes of cocksfoot grass and the drooping false brome. Rising from amid them is a very Surrey-like row of neighbours in rosy brick and tile, dark timber-framing and white plasterwork. Church House is particularly noticeable for its use of grey bricks. They were more expensive as they were in short supply, coming from the outer layer of the stack in the kiln where more oxygen changed their colour. They are nothing compared with the richness of the song of the wrens in the hedge bottom.

The Angel, Guildford

Guildford

Guildford has a noble past – a Saxon mint town, a castle town made the most royal in the realm by King John, a bridge town and canal port, a centre for milling and cloth manufacture, a market town and a railway centre. And now the cathedral and university add to its present status as a busy commercial and social centre.

The High Street, famous for its cobbles, also retains the town's chief monuments – starting with the Royal Grammar School at the top, the Hospital of the Blessed Trinity (Abbot's Hospital), Holy Trinity church, the façade of the Corn Exchange, Guildford House, the Guildhall and its clock, The Angel posting inn and so down to the river.

The Norman castle keep still crowns its bluff above the Saxon church of St Mary, while over the river, on one hill stand the ruins of St Catherine's chapel and on Stag Hill, the cathedral and university.

That's enough to make any explorer tired, especially as the High Street is so steep. It has all filled many guide book pages but the purpose of this book was to draw attention to the lesser known interest. Sadly that is very fragmented in Guildford. The historic heart has been under attack for over a century and little remains to be seen that is of more than local interest. There is no counterpart to Farnham's Castle Street to evoke Georgian times, nor a walk like that along Egham's Hythe to evoke a bridge-point settlement. It is difficult to picture Guildford's long story; just isolated illustrations to a text on the library shelves. Let's begin then outside the library in North Street.

NORTH STREET TO STOKE FIELDS AND BACK
Quakers, firemen, poor widows and coalmen people some of the pauses along this walk through the best of the older surviving parts of Guildford closest to the town centre. A sunny Sunday afternoon when there is least traffic is highly recommended.

A formal public garden hides away between walls at the

top of North Street beside the public library. It is known as Quakers' Acre because this is the site developed by The Society of Friends when their meetings were made legal in the late 17th century. The plot was given to the town in 1927 and makes a pleasant resting place after trudging up the hill.

We'll reach the present Quaker Meeting House in a moment but first note the library which opened in 1961 and is worth a glance for having stood the test of time. It still looks smart and decent while so many of its contemporaries are seriously decrepit. Then comes Jeffreys Passage which is the best of the famous cross links to the High Street. The other two, Market Street and Swan Lane, have been smartened up and lost their former charm.

The long brick building projecting into the street, complete with towered Victorian frontage, is more interesting than it would seem. The main building running back is a cloth hall of 1619 built by Guildford's George Abbot who became Archbishop of Canterbury. It is part of his attempt to revive the town's failing woollen cloth industry but he did not succeed. The building, however, remains the town's best illustration of that trade and an appropriate link with Abbot who was himself the son of a clothworker.

From beside it you can view the back of his greatest monument, the Hospital of the Blessed Trinity, known so often today simply as Abbot's Hospital. These almshouses, in striking Jacobean architecture, are open to the public at certain times, through the imposing front entrance in the High Street.

Cross the road and notice if you glance down the street that there are no other old buildings in view from before the 19th century. That's because the street is relatively new, having been the town ditch previously. Its lack of architectural interest is compensated for on Fridays and Saturdays when the side bustles with activity as the costermongers on their street stalls peddle their colourful wares and maintain an old tradition. Back in the Middle Ages costermongers were named after their wares – their costards or apples.

At the top of the street was the green on which Tudor boys from the grammar school played cricket. That's often quoted as the first written record of the game but is very arguable.

More certain is that at this crossing place was a weighing machine for hay and corn brought up to the edge of the town across Stoke Fields. Now you'll find public lavatories there but in a grand little brick building rising to a little clock tower. This was built as the fire station. It was designed by Henry Peak, Borough Surveyor and a man of local importance.

Behind it, in Ward Street, you'll find the present meeting house of the Society of Friends. It was built plainly, in accordance with Quaker beliefs, in 1805 and is thus one of the county's oldest. Opposite stands the Guildford Institute, founded in 1834 but suffering so many internal wrangles that

Entrance to the Friends' Meeting House, Guildford

this building was not erected until 1892. Rather surprisingly it is not a Gothic Revival effort but domestic classical, smart and dignified, enriched with restrained decorative friezes and ironwork, along this slightly concave Ward Street façade.

For Gothic Revival buildings look next door and there is another at the end of the street. Between these two stone buildings there is room for one building and that, alas, is a red brick modern one; fine enough in itself but not suited to this site. The left-hand 'church' was being cleaned and refurbished at the time of writing and its pale clean stonework was already creating colour harmony with the institute. If the right-hand church could be cleaned too this would be one of the best of Guildford's old streets – except for that red brick intrusion.

The view left from the end reveals a small group remaining from a Victorian terrace backed by a big modern block. Some people hate the modern dwarfing the old, but others will say that here the plainness of the modern deflects the eye down onto the detailing of the Victorian. To the right is an exciting rhythmic terrace, all bow-front, red and white and textured in flint, with pointed doorways. How totally different from the Surrey Advertiser building opposite, with its plain surfaces and rounded corners, all shouting 1930s. It dates from 1936. Until recently it was even more distinctive with a glazed tile front but the tiles became unsafe and had to be removed.

In this grid of short narrow streets it's perhaps easiest to imagine the jostle of Victorian life with dodging delivery boys and rattling horse harness, as the sun picks out the cherry-red brickwork of the house quaintly mis-shapen to fit the corner of Martyr Road. The opposite corner is balanced with a modern version that shows what a little care can achieve. Walk round to the front in Chertsey Street and you'll get a surprise. So did the developers. They found an ancient timber-framed building buried amid later acretions and managed to salvage it. Now, all smartly restored, it nestles alongside its new neighbour in matching brick in a most attractive way.

That new neighbour is good too, in mock Georgian of the 'early' period when they had window frames flush with the walls. Then comes another good modern block, Beaufort

House, attractively planted in front with saplings which this busy street certainly needs – but will there be room for them when they're a little bigger? It's a pity this road is so busy because there are some pleasant enough houses along here, but barely seen as they hide from the dirt and noise behind hedges and walls. Number 2 for example has boldly textured walls of great flint nodules and rhythmic ogee-headed windows; Numbers 9 to 17 are simply Victorian narrow-bay cottages, facing the Regency-style Norfolk House with its low slate roof and columned porch. There is good material all along here but some, like Arundel House (1987) doesn't harmonise. It has a good solid appearance but is in the wrong place. Some of its styling recurs in the 1989 work in Haydon Place where it works to a much greater effect.

Now comes the most exciting of the modern housing (1983) where a section of both sides of the road has been redeveloped in imitation Victorian, endowed with smart, clean-cut modernity and a rich softening of trees and shrubs. A mound of misty blue Ceanothus blossom foams out of the front planter in May and provides just the accent needed. Thoughtful planting has ensured variety and interest all round the site for all the year. Nothing is allowed to be boring; the front elevation is stepped rather than flat, the mass of red brick is relieved with two whitened sections echoed by another opposite, and so on. Some people think they are first rate, while on the other hand a passer-by was heard to comment, 'God, aren't those awful!'

Look next for the wool sack. It's stylised into an inscription stone in the front of one of Guildford's most ignored monuments, Parsons' Hospital. Brothers William and Henry Parsons, wool and linen merchants in the town, endowed these almshouses for six elderly widows. They were built in 1799 in an unbelievably old-fashioned style which explains partly why they are so ignored. They went to all the trouble to crown the centre with that attractive white cupola but did so in a style going back to before their own time. The brickwork too, even with the dignified pedimented centre, looks early 18th century. Only the arched windows give any obvious hint to the oncoming Regency style of their time. All we need is an imaginary glimpse of the old ladies having a

The market at Guildford

gossip beside the street, pulling their special blue gowns closer against the wind.

The road goes on to Stoke (see below) but for this walk turn away from the almshouses to take the path called Stoke Fields diagonally opposite.

Come in May when everyone's efforts to keep trees and shrubs and little front gardens are rewarded down this way. All the old favourites fill the space with colour and scent, from apple blossom and flowering cherry to climbing roses round the door, golden laburnum and lilacs in purple and mauve and white, tall bearded irises and bowing red peonies – super.

Look down too, as you pass the terrace on the right and you'll find a cast iron disc in the paving slab before each front door. They are Victorian coal hole covers! Imagine the coal cart creaking up and grubby little boys in hob-nailed boots trying to shoot coal cleanly down the hole, in the hope of an extra penny, and ignoring the dour warnings not to blacken the spruce front doorway.

At the end you'll reach the old school buildings and have to cross the road via the subway (quite steep for some wheelchair users) and come out to the left to follow Sandfield Terrace towards the red tower on the skyline. The tower belongs to Holy Trinity church at the top of the High Street. Its plain Palladian red-brick tower is not very high but then it didn't need to be when its only tall rival was Abbot's Hospital opposite. Nowadays it still manages to pop into several skyline views as you look along the streets and it thereby contributes a vital accent to the townscaping.

The Nonconformists come onto the scene when you look left from the end of Sandfield Terrace. Across the top of the road stands their Bethel Strict Baptist chapel, built 1910 and surprisingly small and low. It doesn't look much from here but its main front is more attractive closer to, but it hasn't room to show itself off while heeled into this backyard corner.

Walking back down The Bars you'll pass the barracks of England's Senior Infantry Regiment, A Company 5th (Volunteer) Battalion, Queen's Regiment, before turning left into Haydon Place for North Street and the starting point.

STOKE (an extension of the previous walk, from Parsons' Hospital)
Green fields and waterways and things medieval all help to make this a varied addition to any exploration of Guildford, despite its location on a main road junction.

THE CHURCH SIDE (motorists park **before** passing the church)
The delightful chequerwork of flint and stone makes the 15th century church tower unlike any other in Surrey. It is of a style found more regularly in the lower Thames Valley, so obviously an outsider was brought in to build this. That's not so surprising when the advowson was owned by the influential church of St Pancras at Lewes in East Sussex. Much innovation came from there and so it is not so surprising either that this church should have such an unusual east window. The stone mullions rise straight up through the tracery to the arch of the head instead of splaying out to form the heads of the tracery lights.

Inside it has been mostly Victorianised but is still basically 14th century which makes a change in Surrey. Among all the monuments is one to Henry Parsons of the aforementioned hospital and just like his hospital his memorial is old-fashioned by about a hundred years! The earliest monument is of 1610 to John Stoughton, a name familiar for being that of the adjoining district. The manor of Stoughton was in the parish of Stoke.

The district was all very different then – open farmland, and one of the timber-framed farmhouses still stands, in Josephs Road opposite the church. One of the crosswings is dated 1663 but the other wing, close-studded and of differing proportions, is older (probably 16th century). A little further along is another 16th century timber-framed house, contrasting with the other for having white plaster infill instead of the herringbone brickwork. What a surprise these two make in a suburban street!

STOKE MILL, LOCK AND WATERWAYS (beyond the main junction)

Reaching five storeys, Stoke Mill of 1879 cannot be missed. Uncertainties about its future recently provoked an outcry and so it is liable to stay, indeed at the time of writing it was wrapped in plastic sheeting as work was being done on it.

Although the present mill is Victorian there have been mills here for hundreds of years; two were recorded in the Domesday Book (1086). The mill house beside the leet is partly 18th century and for 200 years there was a paper mill alongside too. Paths take you along the waterside to follow the river out through the fields. Another waterway cuts across the meander and this is the Wey Navigation, one of the first long distance canal schemes of England.

It was the brainchild of Sir Richard Weston who had been on a tour of the Low Countries when he was a teenager. Shrewdly he noted how they maximised the economic value of their land and returned with some new ideas, to implement as soon as he could inherit Sutton Place. He didn't have to wait for long. In 1613, aged 22, he inherited. Soon he set about cutting this artificial channel and had Stoke Lock ready by about 1618. It was the first pound lock in Surrey.

Stoke Lock, Guildford

His intention was to overfill the channel so that it would flood over the watermeadows and irrigate them. That would also raise the temperature three degrees, keep the frost off and promote fresh grass early in the spring. Fewer cattle would be lost through lack of adequate food if the winter's hay ran out before the cold drying winds of March let up.

Soon he was allowing the boat traffic on the Wey to use it as a short cut and then of course came the plans to extend the scheme right down the river to the Thames and so link with London docks and world trade. All his life he strove to bring this radical idea to fruition but he died a few months before it was finally opened, in 1653.

Alongside this story is the one that he bought the timber, stone and brick for the locks from one Robert Turbridge. He in turn had amassed them by dismantling the former royal palace of Oatlands at Weybridge. That was the condition imposed upon him by Parliament when he bought it from them. They had confiscated it after the execution of Charles I.

The palace in turn had been built from materials acquired by dismantling Chertsey abbey at the Dissolution of the Monasteries. Here at Stoke there's a large dressed stone built into the lock which is pointed out as evidence for the truth of this story. Whether the stone started life at the palace or the abbey or had been at both is anybody's guess but dallying by the waterside at Stoke is just the place to ponder such things.

MILLMEAD AND AROUND

The High Street runs down to the river Wey which was made navigable as far as this in the mid 17th century. From 1653 boat traffic came up to wharves from Weybridge, the Thames and London Docks. A great clutter of warehousing developed along the banks so we can imagine how devastating was the great flood in February 1900 that swept away the old stone-arched bridge.

Today an elegant single-span replacement sweeps us over the water. It seems so narrow that it's difficult to realise that until recently it was the main road into Guildford. From it, the view has changed too. All signs of the 'port' have gone, except for one small timber-clad building reached by the walkway on the High Street side.

Rescued from its original position and installed here on the former meal wharf, it houses an 18 ft treadwheel to operate the crane attached. Dating from the late 17th century it is only one of three of its type surviving in the country. The idea of men trundling around inside it like hamsters sounds archaic but there are people alive today who remember doing just that.

One of the arguments for canalising the river was to increase commerce when the town's woollen cloth trade was declining. The patron saint of the woollen industry and thus of Guildford, is the patron saint of animals, St Blaise. He is shown on the plaque on the wall by the crane together with St Dunstan, Archbishop of Canterbury. St Dunstan is the patron saint of silversmiths and serves as a reminder that in Saxon times Guildford was a mint town, producing copper coins for Edward the Martyr from AD975-978.

St Nicolas is the patron of the nearby church which was rebuilt in Victorian times. The incumbent then was the hymn-writer, Dr John Monsell, who stumbled while inspecting the new foundations, broke his arm and subsequently died when complications set in. The alternative story, that he fell from the roof, cannot be true as there weren't any walls, let alone a roof, on 9th April 1875 when he fell.

The incident is recorded on a pottery plaque in the church grass facing the river. Inside (a small door rather than the main door is is unlocked at reasonable times) there is ironwork from the foundry of Filmer and Mason. That was operating between 1820 and 1942 on a site over the river where the Yvonne Arnaud Theatre now stands.

The theatre, by local architects Scott, Brownrigg and Turner, opened in 1965 when its design was far too modern for many people's tastes. Now of course they much prefer it to some of its neighbours! The name honours the Guildford actress and musician Yvonne Arnaud (1890-1958) who is buried outside the town at St Martha's-on-the-Hill (her stone is by the gate in the east wall of the churchyard).

Beside the theatre and used by it, is the fine town mill of 1770 with a mid 19th century western extension. It ground corn until 1894 and the profits went to help Guildford's poor. Mills have stood about this site since Saxon times.

Along here the mill pool and the divided river make for attractive dallying or a more rural walk out of town. A footbridge leads over to the watermeadows which are preserved to act as an emergency reservoir in times of flood. Alternatively there is a riverside walk along the towpath since the opening in 1764 of an extension of the navigation from here up to Godalming. A little upstream, walkers can also join the North Downs Way.

Meanwhile there's plenty to see in this small square with its plane trees: the Westnye Gardens, the Baptist Centre (1972) and old houses. Some are deceptive because they have later exteriors but Bow Cottage (circa 1700) at the end will catch the eye. There have been houses along here since at least the 13th century.

From the entrance to the council offices take the alleyway that rises not too steeply to Buryfields. This has returned to its old name of Porridge Pot Alley having been Backhouse Lane between times but that was soon crudely corrupted to

Guildford castle keep

reflect public opinion of its squalor. The name change was to enhance its image and in recent years it has been repaved and smartened again to make it a pleasant walk.

The carefully proportioned Mead Cottage stands opposite the top and is arguably the only cottage in Guildford's centre that is worth going to see. It is simple and smart, built of local stone with white wooden window frames with slightly arched tops to carry a heading of larger stones. It must be Victorian, yet is so difficult to date exactly. That's because it's not the usual builders' job but an architect's little masterpiece.

The date is in fact 1895. The architect was a local man, H Thackery Turner (1853 – 1937) who deserves wider recognition. He had a love and respect for local style and materials which he could manipulate to suit the needs and nature of the project. This point is clearly appreciated by comparing Mead Cottage with his other two works nearby (see below). He was a man who took care. Even this cottage has been given the attention one would expect of a major work – presumably to him it was.

In contrast how stark is the nearby parish hall of 1885. It is the massive red brick building rising behind, now the Guildford School of Art and Dance. Nevertheless, it is just as much an expression of its times. What fun the architect had at playing classical with bricks: stepped gables, ball finials, concave niches, fluted pilasters, balustrading and florid swags to hold the date – everything he could think of, all flung up the great frontage.

Move on northwards along Buryfields to The Court. This has an Elizabethan feel to it, with the long range and cross wings, all creamy-coloured, creating a large central space not as a courtyard but as a garden, rich with the scent of apple blossom and bluebells in Spring. It's not Elizabethan of course but a range of 15 houses; a stately home for those who can't afford one. The date is a problem. There's a 1920s feel about it but the true date is 1902. This is H Thackery Turner again, working ahead of his time. The relationship between scale and proportion shows once more the care that he took over his projects. Textured walls of stone were right for a

Guildford cathedral

small cottage but not for the large surfaces here – they would be fussy. Instead, these are smooth.

All along here there are satisfying minor houses with Number 11 at the end upstaging them all by having a Jacobean coat of royal arms in its 18th century façade. Some of the glass windowpanes are old too.

Then at the road junction with Bury Street there is a particularly satisfying view down to the domestic architecture of Numbers 1 to 3 with the church behind. On the right stands 17th century Westbury House with Dutch gable and Georgian façade and Tuscan porch.

In contrast to this lightly formal dignity, the view left, up Bury Street, is past the long terrace of 17th/18th century Wey Cottages looking rather rustic. At the top is Thackery Turner's third masterpiece, the Wycliffe Buildings. This block of flats, dating from 1894, needs looking at from a variety of angles in order to appreciate how the awkward shape of the site and the fall in ground level were all accommodated into the masterly design.

Walking down into that pleasing view in Bury Street will bring you to the Caleb Lovejoy Almshouses – small and decorative. When their founder died in 1676 he left 14 properties in Southwark to provide money for educating the poor of this parish and to build four almshouses. The money wasn't enough and so not until 1838 was it possible to build this modest block. There is a memorial to Lovejoy in his parish church of St Nicolas, just round the corner, where this exploration began.

Haslemere

Sometimes described as Surrey's most beautiful town, it is really the setting that is so beautiful, up in the hills (the highest point of the railway line) with deep valleys between; still unspoiled with a rich covering of woods and trees, heaths and pastures. The High Street is very distinctive but there is little about the town that is any more beautiful than other Surrey towns.

THE NORTHERN APPROACH AND HIGH STREET

The Haslemere boundary is reached on the A286 at Grayswood with its village green on one side of the road and the church on the other. The latter was built at the very beginning of the 20th century in local materials and local style, so that it looks well in its setting but closer study shows its provincialism.

The road continues up a beautiful valley with views across to Hurt Hill on the Hindhead range while itself flanking Grayswood Hill. On the summit is the large house of 'Grayswood Hill', renowned for its garden. This sandstone outcrop is not the ideal place for a great garden yet rare plants have found a good home here and new ones have been bred, such as the conifer 'Grayswood Pillar'.

Over the brow and the road passes Jesses on the left, the house to which the Dolmetsch family came in 1917. This is the Dolmetsch of early music fame and for repopularising the recorder in particular. Through their efforts the annual Haslemere Festival began in 1925 and continues today, achieving considerable recognition.

Around this route prehistoric peoples lived; their burial urns have been unearthed in Beech Road. The modern settlement is reached at the first cross-roads. Here was once the gate (hatch) to keep the common cattle out of the town, with the pound for strays on the left (see the plaque on the wall by the letter box). Three Gates Lane leads off here. Follow that far enough and the Manor is reached. Not much can be seen through the fine gates but it is one of only five houses in Surrey of good quality Carolean architecture.

On the way Meadfields is passed. This was part of the lands owned by Sir Robert Hunter, co-founder of the National Trust. Next door is Springfold, another notable garden, opened to the public occasionally.

From the pound one enters the town, quite suddenly and unexpectedly. Over the wall on the right was Pound Corner Nursery, the last survivor of several local plant nurseries. There was another in Tanners Lane and Mr Howard's was out along the Petworth Road. They played a significant role. The district was rich in large private houses employing their own gardeners to keep them largely self-sufficient in fruit and vegetables. The wars broke this age-old pattern and it was these nurseries that exploited the situation by rearing vegetable plants to help the fewer and overworked gardeners that remained.

Clarence Birdseye's development of deep freezing as a means of preserving food and creating convenience foods hastened the decline. At first it was exploited, so Haslemere boasted a freezer centre long before such things were generally heard of. One could step off the High Street, through impressive vault-like doors into refrigerated stores where all the local 'big houses' could keep their surplus. This included game that the keepers had reared on the local estates for the shooting season. Bicknell's was the last shop to recall these times, with its open front hung with braces of pheasants, pigeons etc and its cold shelf offering fresh oysters, still half alive.

That was the local lifestyle and one clung to more tenaciously here than anywhere else in Surrey. With that in mind much of the surrounding landscape makes more sense. So does the High Street – where all the big hotels and inns are to be found. Where are the big chain stores?

Accommodation was in only limited demand, for although the district was so renowned for its beauty and healthy air, visitors stayed with their friends at the big houses. The households did their main shopping in London, courtesy of the railway. Going up to town was part of the lifestyle, stifling local developments (not like Staines where Johnson and Clark's Department Store can be traced back to 1790). The first breakthrough came in 1951 with the opening of a branch of F W Woolworth Ltd after considerable opposition. They acquired, and still have, one of the old tile-hung buildings at the top of the High Street next to a barn that had been carefully converted into a china shop. Nothing was to spoil this and so Woolworth's had to agree not to use their familiar red fascia board. Today the letters are still fixed to the tiles.

Opening day brought a queue at the door (an unfamiliar sight in Haslemere) and the first customer received a tea service. They were off! Sweets were bought loose as were bags of broken biscuits. Such items were stored where they would keep freshest – in the flat above, which required assistants trundling off with a basket, out of the front door and up an outside passage between the buildings to reach the flat's entrance. Other goods were stored in garages at the top of a concrete ramp in the back garden. That is where the assistants' bikes went too; anyone late for work had to wheel their bike between the customers in the shop as there was no rear entrance. Then there was the memorable smell, created afresh every Saturday night with the oiling of the wooden floor. Prices remained in farthings longer than the other shops. Roasted salted peanuts were sold, hot from the light bulb of the illuminated dispenser, for ninepence farthing a quarter. The greaseproof paper bag was clutched closely to keep hands warm for the walk home in the winter.

It seems a far cry from today's chain stores but it was ahead of its time in one respect. Out the back they sold boxes of bedding plants, tomatoes etc, something today's supermarkets are striving for, much to the consternation of the garden centres (introduced to England, in Surrey, in 1958). Only one significant change has occurred. Woolworth's no longer sell food in the Haslemere branch. They lost out to the undercutting prices of the small foodmarkets when they arrived. Nevertheless, Woolworth's are still the only major chain store to have conquered Haslemere.

As for the other shops, they catered primarily for everyday needs. People went to Guildford for anything big or special. Livestock went to Guildford market too, so although markets

The Georgian Hotel, Haslemere High Street

were formerly held in the High Street they were never as important as they might have been. Hotels and pubs remained small.

The chief hotel has always been The Georgian, long held to have been the home of General James Oglethorpe, founder of the American State of Georgia, but recently this connection has been disproved. He was the local MP from 1722 to 1754 which sounds more promising. It's not. Haslemere was a 'Rotten Borough' until disfranchised by the 1835 Municipal Reform Act. It had been given borough status in 1584 but only to strengthen royal influence in the House of Commons.

The town hall still stands – the focal point in the High Street but it was not known to Oglethorpe. It was only built in 1814 but again so conservatively that it looks at least as old as his time, if not a generation before. The treed hillside behind makes a perfect backdrop like the downs do behind Guildford High Street.

Although the land rises behind, the High Street is not the lowest point as can be seen from Well Lane, opposite the Georgian Hotel, where there is a startling view down into a deep valley of fields and woods. Haslemere is then seen to be perched on its lip. Amazingly the valley hasn't been developed. The secret of that lies with The National Trust to whom it was willed in 1954-55 to protect its beauty. A signposted footpath from the Petworth Road takes walkers down through the valley, through old coppices, out past the Meadfield lands of Sir Robert Hunter to Holdfast. More paths push on to Chiddingfold via the hammer ponds of the former ironworks at Imbhams.

A walk round the High Street reveals little of note. The mid 18th century is represented by the Palladian façade to the White Horse, and earlier in the century Town House was built and that's the one with tales to tell.

Local traditions, attributed to a number of parishes, recall a cleric whose cassock sometimes bulged over what looked suspiciously like pistol butts, a cleric who always ended services on those occasions with long hymns – long enough for him to defrock in the vestry and to ride off on his horse kept tethered outside. People began to think he was a highwayman, after all his standard of living was high for a cleric, but then again he was also the local magistrate and just as vexed by the local robberies as anyone else.

The Haslemere version of this story links the gentleman with Town House where the Rev James Fielding lived circa 1772-84. He died in 1817 and soon slipped from people's thoughts until, that is, later renovations to Town House involved lifting the floorboards. There they discovered a cache of 18th century mail bags complete with brass identity tags.

Highwayman's house, Haslemere

The Rev James Fielding had been buried at Haslemere's parish church of St Bartholomew in an unmarked vault, probably under what is now the main path. The church stands well away from the town centre and to reach it the cleric would have crossed another valley with pools, marshes and mill ponds. They all went when it was decided to drive the railway through this natural cutting. Tanners Lane remains as a reminder of earlier activities here.

The church area is not unattractive with its sloping green, planted long ago with horse chestnut trees, backed by the large early 18th century Church Hill House. To the north the church rooms are housed in the former church school: a little Gothic building that would complement the scene so much more if its old play areas were enhanced. Between them stands the church, rebuilt in 1871. Ignore its description as 'hopeless' until you've seen it for yourself. The long chancel with tall narrow lancet windows demonstrates more clearly the 13th century stereotype than any of the originals surviving in Surrey.

At the west end the original tower was retained. It is so devoid of detail it is difficult to date, but is probably 13th century. It is more like a defensive refuge tower and indeed that may well have been in its builders' minds for in those days it was a chapel of Chiddingfold, lost out in the remote forested hills, not the securist place to live.

The interior is not a Victorian glory except perhaps in its hopelessness. The font in gaudy coloured marble says it all as soon as you enter but says it more brazenly than any other in the county. The stained glass doesn't merit comment either although one window in the north aisle, designed by Burne-Jones, attracts visitors because it is a memorial to the local Poet Laureate, Alfred, Lord Tennyson.

The Nonconformists aren't without interest. Tradition has it that they began meeting on Shepherds Hill that runs out of the south-west corner of the High Street and here regular preaching began in 1792. It was a difficult struggle. In 1815 the Rev D Evans would only accept the pulpit for one year, fearing 'the spirit of Antinomianism prevailing amongst the people'. He did stay longer, having decided that a strict moral code should be enforced for the good of the people's

Stone Tudor cottage at Haslemere

souls. Enforced it was. People missing three meetings had to account for themselves in public and if answering unsatisfactorily were roundly reproved from the pulpit. Similarly, a ferocious public humiliation was brought down on anyone 'prattling' about others and to make sure no one escaped there was a duty to report weaknesses in members so that all the others could 'do their duty accordingly'.

Not surprisingly this caused a division of the members in 1818. Evans had his supporters though and they worked on. He didn't leave until 1830. The church prospered sufficiently to plan the building of a new chapel which was begun in 1882 and soon opened 'with great rejoicing and practically free from debt, two friends having agreed to guarantee any deficiency'. It stands below Shepherds Hill at the beginning of Lower Street.

Further along Lower Street a scarce William and Mary style house was saved (a little altered) but the nearby blacksmith's was not. The smithy has been partially reconstructed in the town's famous museum. Then there's Yew Tree Cottage, nestling into the hillside. It is genuine 17th century work in the local tradition that the Victorians loved so much and reproduced by the thousand. This one was the subject of a Helen Allingham painting. Further on, near the station is a Surrey rarity – a small Tudor house built of stone. It has pleasing proportions and a satisfying alternation of large and small windows, complete with hoodmoulds. Somebody was obviously doing well when this was a new borough sending two members to Parliament.

Hersham & Whiteley

HERSHAM

Try Hersham on a sunny Sunday afternoon when the gardens are golden with daffodils. The yellow London stock brick of the Victorian housing glows warmly and shows how the streets developed in the 19th century. A great deal more is of a later date but there is not much in the worst styles of the 1960s; development was concentrated at that time upon neighbouring Walton. Here at Hersham the latest buildings have often reverted to yellow brick to give more continuity and harmony than might otherwise be the case.

THE PARISH CHURCH AND VAUXMEAD

The parish church is often a good place to collect clues for understanding a new place. Hersham's has some surprises. Its oak-shingled spire with chamfered edges is in good South-Eastern style but when you arrive you find it is Victorian as indeed is everything you can see from the outside. Someone tried to re-create the development of a medieval church by varying the fenestration styles from Lancets through to plate and geometric tracery. That someone was J L Pearson who was responsible for the fine tower on Weybridge church not so far away. This at Hersham is nearly 40 years further on (1887) and the rest of the outside lacks distinction.

Step inside, however, and the volumes have been created well. Here again it's all Victorian, suggesting Hersham is largely a product of those times. The size of the church suggests it must have been quite a flourishing community too. Having found that the tower stands off the north-west corner with the main entrance porch through it, one wonders what other quirks lie beyond. Visitors step into a traditional scene though, with fine Early English style arcades balancing the proportions between nave and aisles.

The walk down the aisles is within cool walls of tastefully whitened brick and then there's the chancel screen – a spidery metallic thing – and there beyond is that expected surprise. The rather dark chancel has all its wall surfaces decorated with patterns and figures. The colours have darkened, the lighting is low, it's a wonderland of Victoriana. A finely carved stone reredos behind the altar completes the scene.

Look around and one wonders where all the money came from as there are no great monuments to Victorian benefactors. Indeed there are incredibly few memorials at all and not much of a display of stained glass either. So how did all this come about? A clue lies opposite the church as you leave by the herringbone brick path (notice the weeping beech in the corner, a type of tree originated in Surrey in 1820). It is simply a field, the Vauxmead. This nearly became the site of the new church when the expanding Victorian community outgrew the old one. Then, however, it was realised that moving across the road to a larger site would be a financial folly because burials at the old site would preclude it being sold off. The solution would be to acquire land adjoining the old site and enlarge it.

It just so happened that the owner of the adjoining farm was being forced to sell up by the courts to pay off a debt of £121 17s 6d owed to a gardener. While all this was going on the commissioned architect, Sir Arthur Blomfield, became fully occupied building the London Law Courts and had no time for little places like Hersham. Pearson got the job instead.

The new church still cost more than the villagers could afford and so a local landowner was forthcoming. He was the lawyer Francis Bircham of the Burhill Estates to the south of the village. He gave £3,270. Unfortunately the project took so long to reach fruition that he had been dead several years before the new building was ready for consecration, but his house in the park played its part. There, on Consecration Day, the bishop was entertained by its new hostess, the Dowager Duchess of Wellington. There was also a royal contingent on that day for the foundation stone had been laid the year before by HRH the Duchess of Albany from nearby Claremont. She and her court were entertained, not with the bishop, but at Hersham's other great house by the church, Burvale, by Colonel Terry and his wife. There was a third gathering, at the vicarage, for the most important of all – the workmen.

THE SCHOOL AND THE GREEN

Turning northwards from Vauxmead the visitor cannot miss the fine big range of the village school. It is now much larger than the little building with accommodation for a single teacher that William Shearburn of Dorking was commissioned to build in 1842.

The school was established by the Anglican members of the community and so they naturally turned to their Church for guidance on the matter – The National Schools' Society. The trouble with that was the society's stipulation that each school day must include religious education according to the principles of the Church of England.

Such a notion caused little trouble for most of Surrey, where dissenting Nonconformists were a minority voice in village affairs. They were left to do without or provide their own schools. At Hersham things were rather different. Not ever having been a very grand place it attracted many Nonconformists who found they could live and worship here without offending the Anglicans centred on the surrounding towns. They became more than a minority group. On Sunday 30th March 1851 a census of the congregations was taken, thought to be the only official census of its kind. It showed there were 436 Anglicans and 367 Nonconformists. The latter had built their own schoolroom and were not concerned about the Anglican provision.

That was alright until the 1870 Education Act made more demands upon each group than either could afford. Hersham wasn't alone in this and so the Government established school boards in poorer districts which could raise the money required by levying a school rate. Foreseeing that households would not comply with helping to educate different denominations from their own, the Government instructed the boards to operate schools on a non-denominational basis.

The factions in Hersham would not agree to this. They continued raising their own funds and to continue without the help of any such board but they failed. In 1875 they were forced to give in and turn to a school board for aid. Ah, but the story doesn't end there. The crafty folk of Hersham exploited the Act to their advantage. If religious instruction (non-denominational) was to be the first or last lesson of the day then the Trustees would only lease the school buildings to the board from 10am. That gave the vicar an hour to nip in and teach Anglicanism because that was the faction that had most members as trustees.

As you can imagine the Nonconformists weren't too pleased about this. They worked to get a majority among the trustees and when they did 'scenes of tumult and insubordination broke out.' Oh, if only they'd known that in due course it would become a Roman Catholic school! Still, as we stand in the road we can still read a stone up in the gable that records the Anglican days: 'Added to the Hersham National Schools by the bounty of John Davies Middleton Commander RN and Harriett his wife MDCCCLXVIII.'

When it comes to the green beside the school it is clear once again that Hersham folk have been a very principled lot. While the arguments raged over the schools there was further division over the green. Beside the school runs Faulkner Road and it was one of Mr James Faulkner's bright ideas that caused the row. He suggested that a field next to the green should be bought by public subscription and held by trustees as a public open space. Great! They did it. Then he suggested that the dividing hedge be removed. That would mean merging the public green, awarded to the poor by the Enclosure Act, with land now held by the trustees of the field. That would never do. The field remained hedged as a recreation ground.

Today the green is a pleasant space amid all the development. It hasn't been hemmed in by big modern blocks but is largely lined with small homes. The view does somehow remind one of the closeness of London, especially with the plane trees, and even the Watermans Arms looks more outer London than village pub, but that's all part of the variety of Surrey.

THE DEVELOPING STORY
Exploring the district, it is easy to overlook the fact that the site of Hersham lies on the ridge between the last few miles

of the rivers Wey and Mole before they join the Thames. Up on the southern bluff (St George's Hill) prehistoric people had built a fort but from then on communities preferred permanent settlements along the rivers, creating Weybridge, Walton and Cobham and leaving the upland areas to peasant economy.

Thus, in due course, it was possible to create large country estates, from Painshill in the south to Claremont in the north, with Burhill and Burwood over the lands between. The peasants were left to exploit the heathlands as best they could and very poor they were too. Their homes were built of dried-out mud and Hersham's 'Mudtown' persisted right up to the Second World War when a bomb destroyed most of it and the rest had to be cleared.

At the beginning of the 20th century the demand for land near London and the cost of maintaining vast country estates caused the release of some of the land for modern development. Then the First World War finally broke the traditional social system here as elsewhere and modern Hersham really got under way. A key location was on the Brooklands estates beyond St George's Hill where Hugh Locke King had built his famous race-track, quickly followed by an airfield. These sites attracted associated companies and so cars and planes founded the major local industries. With the coming of the First World War the Brooklands site was taken over by the Government, the Vickers Aircraft Factory there was expanded and lesser companies had to move out.

One was the ABC Motor Company and that moved to Hersham (the ABC stood for All British Company) and many famous cars were made here. The most famous association was with their John Harper Bean of Bean cars fame, but they were also important in the aircraft industry and in due course were taken over by Vickers who closed them down. The site became the Riverdene Trading Estate.

After the war the third major industry was attracted to the area – the Hackbridge and Hewittic Companies exploiting the expansion of the electricity industry. High voltage transformers were needed wherever this exciting new energy source was being adopted and the production of these became the next Hersham speciality.

Unfortunately, these and lesser companies were draining the district of workers and outsiders couldn't be encouraged in because there was nowhere for them to live. So it's after about 1925 that the residential areas came into being. In true Hersham style nothing went very smoothly at first, resulting in the Walton District Council buying out the problem and having the first local council housing, along Molesey Road.

WHITELEY VILLAGE IN THE BURHILL ESTATES

The private parkland of the Burhill Estates prevented Hersham growing southwards to the river Mole. Today, members of the golf club get fine views of the house as they play the greens set out among the ancient oaks. These remains of the old parkland landscape are quite a surprise hereabouts, but within the estates is also an even greater surprise in the private village of Whiteley.

It is composed entirely of almshouses and their amenities – the largest collection in the country. In recent years Europe has seen the founding of several villages specifically for the care of those with special needs but this one was initiated right back in 1907 (building began in 1914). By that time a Victorian nobody had made his proverbial rise to fame and fortune and set aside a million pounds to build a retirement village for 350 'veterans of industry'. It was to be a place of calm and beauty so that they could have a 'quiet and happy time' after their long working lives and that is just what it is.

This astonishing benefaction came from the man who pioneered big department stores – William Whiteley, the 'Universal Provider'. His story and portrait are set out on the monument to Industry in the centre of the village, the work of Sir George Frampton. It was just the right time to plan a peaceful community for the garden city idea was fresh and exciting, so six top architects were invited to submit plans. The winner was Frank Atkinson.

That he planned something special is sensed immediately the privileged visitor passes through great iron gates between Atkinson lodges to start the journey down a fine avenue deep into the park, to a shady pool bridged by Atkinson and so up to a gently sloping hillside. Over the slopes is spread the village.

Instead of the curving tree-lined streets of other garden city inspirations, this one is seen on the map to be a close community planned on an octagon. How misleading maps can be! That rigid grid has to be looked for by visitors to the site because the overwhelming impression is of groups of housing scattered over the slopes between specimen trees and grassy glades, surrounded by protective woodland. The 225 acres of the park were exploited well.

The homes not only make varied groups but show great variety in themselves. This is because Atkinson didn't design all of them (West Avenue is his), for the Trustees invited a further seven top architects to join the project. Thus the Blomfield family are back in Hersham's story: Sir Reginald this time, to build North Avenue (he's perhaps better known for Lambeth Bridge). Sir Aston Webb, having recently completed the façade of Buckingham Palace came to design The Green, the clubhouse, village hall, clock tower etc. The Nonconformist church is his too, while the Anglican church is by Walter Tapper in a style developed about 1300. It looks very much a homely village church tucked, as it is, away back among the trees.

It captures what is special about Whiteley – the impression of natural simplicity. The top architects didn't turn it into a showground; these were not great public works with which to vie with each other. Here they could be modest and sincere. They were not aiming to create great architecture but to fulfil a great idea.

Horley

AROUND THE CHURCH

One Ralph Salaman was the man of importance here in the early Middle Ages. His manor, according to one of the village stories, didn't have a proper church and graveyard but a large mound in which the villagers interred their dead. Ralph didn't like the prospect of his own bones being scattered when the mound was opened later for the next burial so he built a little chapel by the side, in which he was to be buried.

That mound is the present raised churchyard and Ralph's chapel is now the north aisle of the parish church. In it Ralph was indeed buried, about 1315. The story, appealing as it is, simply explains by myth the raised ground and the north aisle being older than the church. It is highly unlikely to be true.

Village life would have been well organised long before the time of Ralph and that would have included a church and graveyard. Ralph probably built his personal manorial aisle onto an existing church which was later (circa 1400) demolished to make way for a wider finer church which is now the nave.

The fact that Horley is not recorded in the Domesday Book (1086) doesn't necessarily indicate that it is a late settlement. Quite a number of other places deep in the Weald were omitted also, for a variety of reasons. Horley was certainly well established by the time of Ralph because one of his villagers rose to fame as William Hurley. That may come from Hurley in Berkshire but an early spelling as Horley suggests that this was his native village. At his craft he was a genius.

Usually described as a master carpenter, William Hurley could also turn to being a structural engineer, using timber as his raw material. To his carpentry are ascribed the magnificent choir stalls at Ely Cathedral but up above them his engineering is so astounding, even to modern eyes, that it's worth describing in his honour.

In 1322 the central tower of Ely Cathedral collapsed and

gave the sacrist a major problem. To rebuild on the unstable foundations was obviously unwise but this sacrist was the great Alan of Walsingham and soon his imagination was at work. He would create a glorious centre to the cathedral by enlarging the space under the tower into a great room to house the choir. The masons were horrified. It would be 74 ft across and way beyond their capabilities to roof with a stone vault. Walsingham called in the country's greatest carpenter, the king's carpenter, William Hurley. Together they planned the wide octagonal choir complete with a vaulted roof – in wood.

That still left the problem of the central tower. Now the masons were pointing out that the eight pillars of the octagonal choir would be set too far back to use them to build up a tower. Hurley had a stunning idea: he would suspend a great octagonal lantern in mid air! From the eight pillars he would raise 16 struts to support eight wooden pillars to be capped and encased by the lantern, all 400 tons of it.

Fortunately Walsingham had imagination and the plan was agreed. For £8 a year Hurley masterminded the building of his 'castle in the air'. Just winching up the eight pillars was a supreme achievement; they are 63 ft long and three ft thick. Up they all went and fitted so precisely that today, seven centuries later, the beautiful octagon is still suspended 94 ft above the floor of Ely Cathedral.

It is not entirely surprising that Horley should foster great carpenters when we consider its position deep in the Wealden forest. Timber-framed farms were built so soundly that they still stand dotted around the town. That is true right across Surrey to the Hampshire border and Woolmer Forest. There, near Farnham, is the village of Dippenhall and it was Robert de Dippenhall who was employed by the king to build a new chamber at Westminster, a chamber which Hurley roofed for him in 1342. From Farnham too came the country's other genius carpenter, William Herland. It was he who spanned Westminster Hall and showed the world how to roof a space greater than the length of a tree trunk. It was he too who succeeded as the king's chief carpenter on the death of William Hurley in 1354.

At Horley church they tried their own master carpentry by

inserting squared-up tree trunks to support a timber belfry and spire at the west end of Salaman's aisle. That was about 1400. Salaman was already under the floor with a stone monument over the top. When that was later moved to the east end the spot was marked by the inscription on the adjoining column.

Salaman's monument is a typical knight carved in stone but is important for being one of only two such stone monuments in Surrey. The other is the priest at West Horsley but that is a very poor thing compared with all the carved detail rendered in the local Reigate stone of this one. The double-headed eagle is still clearly emblazoned on the shield to tell us it is a Salaman, as do the leopard heads on his shoulders.

Glance up at the windows of the aisle and you'll see in the tops the same golden leopard faces in red surrounds. These are the only surviving lights of medieval glass in the church. The trefoils that house them are upside down – a Kentish variant on the usual design, yet probably sponsored by Chertsey Abbey over in the west of the county for the abbey took over the church in 1313. Presumably local craftsmen from over the nearby Kent border were employed to do the work. These, incidentally, are Victorian replicas of the originals. Salaman must have had plenty of money and influence to build his own chapel, employing craftsmen from one of the country's leading abbeys, and then enrich it with personalised stained glass and his own great monument.

Maybe it is one of the Salaman ladyfolk who stares boldly from her memorial brass on the chancel north wall. Her dress is of particular interest to costume enthusiasts and for added interest she declares her Lancastrian loyalties by wearing their special collar. It is the very complete canopy round the figure, however, that raises this brass to national importance. Notice also, down at the bottom left there was once a little brass to her only son. He would have been standing on her dress, which occurs on only a couple of other brasses.

Below is an inscription but it's a later addition. The Joan Fenner it refers to is not the lady above. Maybe, as some people think, she was the wife of the unnamed civilian on the brass opposite. He is much more appealing and stirs the imagination because he's late enough (circa 1510) to have known the earliest houses still standing in Horley. One of them might even have been his.

Certainly he had the money to afford a quality timber-framed house. The engraver has indicated wealth by turning outwards the gown to reveal its costly fur lining, with no expense spared as it spreads out over the collar. There, below his hands, half his money bag pokes into view. That would have been well and truly hidden, from the muggers on the streets of London where this man must surely have been a merchant. There was little scope for money-making in rural Horley but it was a good place on the main London highway for a country estate.

He would have known the Six Bells next to the church. That was built as an open-hall house about 1450. It shows well the features of such a house and looks particularly rustic under its roof of rough Horsham slabs. Much more unusual is High House adjoining the churchyard because it has hardly been altered since it was built in the early 17th century. We can see how the roof was extended down low towards the ground at the back to increase the internal space; something you'll find in the text books as a 'cat-slide roof'.

In the churchyard a large number of mature Irish yews makes this the best churchyard collection in the county. One of our native yews, once massive but now severely pruned, has been shading the western side for long enough to have protected one of the headstones from the weather so that it shows how beautifully a local craftsman could cut his lettering. Crisp and stylish, it still records the burial of Mr John Charrington in 1772 (early for Surrey stones). More striking is the bold pink mausoleum in polished granite that serves the Parsons family.

The Parsons are remembered as being meat merchants; there was an important trade between the London meat markets and the Wealden cattle farms. Bernard Parsons still makes an unexpected appearance in church for his likeness was re-created in the stained glass window at the east end of the Salaman aisle. There in the right-hand light, below the elbow of Christ, a clean-shaven gentleman looks out. That's Bernard. He's unusual for being clean-shaven at that time and for being represented in a donor window. The Church was frowning upon such depictions and only discovered what was going on when Bernard was already portrayed but they did manage to have the rest of the Parsons family removed from the design.

On leaving church, notice on the north doorway the date 1635 inscribed several times. It is thought that was the work of people who had fled the Great Plague in London. How remote and unfamiliar this scenery must have seemed to them. They would have looked out from here over a great common, nearly a mile square or as big as their City of London. The paths and tracks that criss-crossed it have since been developed as residential roads and that is why the older parts of Horley seem so stretched out. They're round the edge of the common and over its other side at the mill.

ABOUT THE TOWN: RAILWAYS, BREWERY AND BAKEHOUSE
The journey from the church towards the railway station is through some of the later development that became possible after the common was enclosed in 1812. The present town centre, to the north, grew up around the crossing of the tracks over the common.

This southern part followed later but don't despair at any thought of boring residential suburbia. The garden trees and shrubs along the route are not only beautifully mature but the total of different species and cultivars will keep the enthusiast counting for hours.

The station's cherry red brick announces an early 20th century date and sure enough, there on the left-hand gable is the date stone inscribed 1905. The right-hand gable bears, in a smart pedimented frame, an initialled design out of LBSCR – London, Brighton and South Coast Railway. Peering down from this elevated site reveals a great confusion of former trackways all around the existing line. Horley was obviously an important junction once upon a time.

This level site, with water to hand in the river Mole and midway between London and Brighton, caught the eye of the engineers who were seeking a site for a railway works. Here was planned the largest railway centre south of Croydon but reality fell short of these early intentions. Much carriage and engine work was carried out at Horley but for two phases its sidings were better known as the last resting place of geriatric locos. Quite a lot of the site remains to intrigue the industrial archaeologist.

The present station is not the original. That was up beside the present High Street (then known appropriately as Station Road) but it required two level crossings which soon became inconvenient with increased road traffic.

Near here a tall red-brick chimney rises above the rooftops beside the railway footbridge from today's Station Road. This was the Albert Brewery, built about 1869 and extended in 1890, to serve local needs. No doubt the railway workers created quite a demand. Certainly it caught the eye of one of the bigger brewing companies and so in 1904 it was bought up by the Croydon company of Page and Overton. During the First World War it was closed and it never re-opened.

Northwards again and Balcombe Road is reached – a former trackway over the common that got upgraded into a turnpike in 1809. At the top is The Chequers on the A23. This was formerly an important coaching inn on the Brighton run where the mail coaches changed horses. Normally five minutes was allowed for such a stop but it was a matter of pride that changing the horses could be accomplished in one minute or less. Then the landlord's girls would be quickly gathering back the drinking glasses and the guard, resplendent in scarlet livery and high black boots, would be climbing back on top, to his box of firearms. He would sound his horn to clear the road (it was an offence to hinder the Royal Mail) and they would be off again.

Concentrate upon modern traffic as you cross the A23 to The Chequers to enter Horley Row beside it. This road developed out of the track that ran along the top of the Common so you'll find five of the eight original houses still snuggled in among the modern, if you look hard. There's Benhams and Hutchins from the days of open-hall houses and two more oldies at the bottom of Yew Tree Close.

Before that, step into Bakehouse Road and you soon get a view to the left of the Old Bakehouse: a typical 17th century Surrey cottage of brick and tile but with half projecting chimney to give space inside for the bread oven. These are

Old Mill Cottage, Horley

misleading buildings. Bread ovens were a regular feature of farmhouse architecture but all too often today they prompt owners into thinking their property was once a public bakehouse and calling it such. In reality a public bakehouse was not such a common feature of village life as we might imagine. People were expected to bake their own bread and did. There was prejudice against buying someone else's bread. Even in Lancashire today they still have the expression that anyone talking rubbish is 'talking off shop bread'!

THE MILL END OF HORLEY
Horley Row runs into Lee Street and towards its end there is another small collection of timber-framed houses that comprised the other focal point after the church. The two can be reached in dry weather by a footpath over the fields beside the river.

130

Since the early 13th century the village corn mill was driven by the river Mole running through here. That service continued in its time-honoured way until the late 19th century when Horley, like countless other small mills, had to face stiff opposition. Huge flour-milling factories were being built on the waterfronts of the ports where the big new cargo ships docked. Hundreds of tons of grain were being unloaded and promptly processed, more cheaply than ever before. Small local mills had to get modern or get out of the business. Horley was one of these. It was still manorial and the lords of the manor, Christ's Hospital, declined to invest in new machinery and so the mill declined, decayed and finally, in 1924, was demolished.

The mill house still stands, hiding its ancient timbers behind a Victorian frontage. This once served as the village shop, selling everything from funerals to clothing, hardware to furniture, and that gave the shop boy big ideas. His name was John Maple and he went off to London to expand the simple service into the great department store that bears his name.

Over the road, on the corner of Mill Close, stands a pair of Victorian cottages (Numbers 144/146) with a clump of trees beside them. Push through the little iron gate into the undergrowth and you're in the old burial ground of the first Baptist community. That began in a little wooden chapel here on 29th October 1846. There were just seven members.

By 1892 they had increased and flourished sufficiently to be opening, on 5th October, a new substantial chapel over in the town centre. Today this old site, founded on hope and promise, is a sad and forgotten corner, overgrown and vandalised, the headstones smashed off at ground level and the pieces thrown in a heap. Enigmatically, names like George and William cross over their fragment from nettle to nettle and someone called Comber died aged 20.

Nearby is the footpath back to the church, along by the river. The Mole, despite its length across Surrey, remains relatively unknown with few walks along its course. Its waters here, striped with reed grass and dappled with yellow water lily leaves, will encourage more explorers to dally a while.

Leatherhead

Drinkers in The Swan, on 8th October 1806, rushed to the door at the sound of a traffic accident outside. A coach had taken the bend too fast and overturned, flinging its lady passengers into the road in an undignified heap of skirts. Rescuers found one, Harriet Cholmondeley, to be dead. (There is a memorial to her in the church.) Among the survivors they found none other than Princess Caroline, the separated wife of the Prince Regent (later George IV). She was on her way to visit the local notables, the Lockes, at Norbury Park on the downs to the south of the town.

Visitors can still enjoy Norbury Park for much of it is administered by the county council as an Open Space. It consists of glorious woodland and farmland falling over the chalk escarpment into the deep cutting of the river Mole, with climbs up to Box Hill beyond. The ancient bridge town of Leatherhead lies at the northern end of the most beautiful stretch of the Mole valley. There are valley and downland walks all around, and interesting villages to visit, but pause a while in Leatherhead itself.

Many famous people already have. Is this Jane Austen's model for Highbury in *Emma*? Certainly she visited her godfather, the Rev Samuel Cooke, when he was vicar at neighbouring Great Bookham and her characters named Randall and Knightley had real life counterparts in the town's history.

Randalls can be traced back to the Randolphs of early medieval times. One is said to have been a favourite of Edward II and been given lands around Leatherhead as a reward. Much more likely is the connection with the Ranulf recorded here in William the Conqueror's Domesday Book. Twenty years earlier, when William and his men invaded, they spared this district from destruction, for adjoining Fetcham was held personally by Queen Edith. All her lands were spared, helping to substantiate William's claim that her family promised him the throne after the death of her husband, Edward the Confessor.

Saxon times were brought to light again in 1985 when archaeologists were able to excavate part of a Saxon burial ground at a site to be redeveloped by the Esso Petroleum Company. They found 17 interments of Saxon men, women and children of the early Pagan days (6th-7th centuries). Then there was a further and very distinct set of at least 13 adult males, some with their hands tied behind their backs; two had been beheaded. This looked like an execution site and a pit might well have once held the gallows. These record a later Christian phase (AD 700-1200). The end of that brings us well into the times when men of this district of Copthorne met for the Hundred Court at Leatherhead. It has also been distinguished as the seat of the County Court. Thus the settlement is not just old but has been important.

Little survives to remind us of that. The Leatherhead of today is surprisingly compact, making the choice of parking places limited. There's also a tortured one-way system which makes exploring the town by car difficult. The following itinerary is best followed on foot.

THE STATION AND RIVERSIDE

When Sherlock Holmes travelled through Leatherhead station to assist Helen Stoner in *The Speckled Band* it was the same station as stands today. Climbing up the rise to the forecourt presents a view of the patterned brickwork of varying levels, including a low tower block. A closer view shows splendid decorative cast iron supports to the open frontage, reflecting not the low rural status of the little Victorian town but the self-esteem of the railway company as it strove to up-stage its rivals. The first service provided by the new railway was for itself, bringing in these new mass-produced materials for building, from the cast iron units to the Welsh roofing slates. The station opened in 1868 and is the finest early station surviving in Surrey. Hopefully, enough people will appreciate this fine period piece to ensure preservation.

From the station hill follow the road ahead over the crossroads until it turns left under a railway bridge and then right, down Waterway Road, to the river.

Sitting proudly in the junction of Bridge Street and

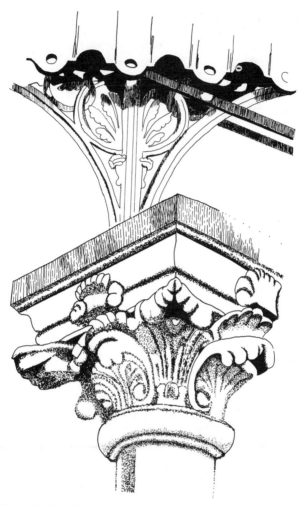

Two details of Victorian railway architecture at Leatherhead

Waterway Road is the finest of the Water Board buildings. Dated 1935, it is boldly self-assertive as one would expect of the best architecture of that time. It is totally plain, relying for its impact upon the subtleties of proportion rather than decoration. This style is not especially fashionable at present and so the relatively few good examples in Surrey could easily be lost and break the visual evidence in the county's building tradition. (The Surrey Herald building in Chertsey has been demolished recently. It was not a very good example but the only one in the whole town).

To the west of the waterworks, the river bridge affords a close view of another example of bold, honest architecture. It is the railway viaduct. This massive structure with four great arches is built of red brick laid in 'English Bond', that is, courses of bricks long-ways between courses laid side-ways. Recently part of its concrete ornamentation has decayed and fallen, but above that the parapet still shows its original detailing with piercings to lighten its appearance. Just as impressive is its reflection in the river below, when there is good light. In addition, a second viaduct a little further downstream, can be viewed, reflections and all, through the arches of the first. Again it is of red brick with four arches, but if you take the riverside path down to it, (not suitable for wheelchairs) then you will find it is in fact slightly but definitely built on a curve.

From the bridge another path follows the river, behind the waterworks, to the Town Bridge (from where there is wheelchair access). It is now a good few years since the buildings were cleared from this site and the banks planned as an attractive riverside walk. What happened to all those good intentions? Is an open space, a strip of hard path and some mown grass the best that can be achieved? Leatherhead has few corners which are restful and beautiful; this could so easily have been one of them.

From here there are views of the Town Bridge, built in 1782 but not of fine Georgian architecture (there are only two old bridges of note in the county – Chertsey and Staines). Instead, this bridge speaks more loudly of its place and time; simple vernacular architecture for a small agricultural town. It stretches over no less than 14 arches, a sweeping causeway across the old watermeadows bringing the Guildford road to the foot of the town on its shoulder of ground above the flood levels.

Local tradition has it that in days before this bridge, the floods prevented Elizabeth I travelling this way and she was forced to spend the night in The Running Horse which still stands by the town end of the bridge. I don't know of it being

The Town Bridge, Leatherhead

proved but she almost certainly passed by it, to reach Manors like Slyfield, and so perhaps she paused here for one of those entertainments that the people provided all along her 'progress' routes. The Running Horse is believed to be that referred to by Henry VIII's Poet Laureate, Skelton, as the noted ale house of Elynour Rumminge.

Opposite, Minchin Close continues as a path through the gardens of the Mansion and so to the Dorking road. It's a more countrified walk but a steep rough climb for wheelchairs at the end. The Mansion is the finest town house in Leatherhead; a bold classical block rebuilt about 1740 and now the county library. A resident of an earlier house was Sir Thomas Bludworth who was Lord Mayor of London at the

136

time of the Great Fire. His daughter was taken by the notorious Judge Jeffreys as his second wife.

In the earlier house Elizabeth I dined on 3rd August 1591, guest of her Master of the Revels, Edmund Tilney. He was also, in his will, a benefactor of the town. Another resident may well have been Robert Cheeseman to whom the house was given by Henry VIII. Cheeseman is portrayed by Hans Holbein the Younger as a yeoman falconer to the king but served him also as one of the squires who escorted Anne of Cleves into the country and he was a grand juror at the trials of Catherine Howard and Cardinal Wolsey.

Before crossing over to the church, turn right and down the hill to turn right again. A lane crosses the river Mole and affords views across lawns to another smart classical house, mainly of 1772. This is a rebuilding of the ancient important Manor of Thorncroft. At its left end is a very modern office block but it doesn't mar this green and leafy parkland at all. Its camouflage is practically total. That is achieved by the simple, but no doubt expensive, expedient of creating the box almost entirely of mirror glass, so all one sees is more trees and a space of sky. Walk on up the lane for a closer view. The glass duplicates an attractive white estate house beside it and, in the winter, an interlace of twigs against the sky of weak sunlight. This, surely, is the way to exploit modern technology.

Among the holders of the earlier manor house was Robert Gardiner, another of Elizabeth I's servants. He was her Sergeant of the Wine Cellar and there is a monument to him in the church (see below). The same office was held by another Leatherhead man, Richard Dalton, for Charles II. The whole district provided many royal court servants, often for generation after generation, as was the case with the Daltons.

THE CHURCH
The church, on a bluff above the river, has a massive late medieval tower in the Perpendicular style. Although there are countless windows and other small examples of this style in the county there is little on a large scale so it is surprising that this tower should be so often ignored. It's finer than West Molesey's but not such good quality as Stoke-by-Guildford.

Leatherhead's large medieval church rarely gets a mention. Admittedly it has been so restored as to remove most of its character but it's not without beauty or interest.

Both beauty and interest can be found just inside the door, in the north-west window. It contains eight roundels of medieval stained glass, not original but created out of surviving fragments, from a wide span of time. Nevertheless, the fragments are large enough to show the mastery of line of the early artists in some of the faces. Also present are striking

Medieval stained glass in Leatherhead parish church

examples of the colours at their disposal; you can't miss the deep rich intensity of their ruby red nor the deep translucence of the blue. Presumably it was the golden glowing demon's head that brought Hieronymus Bosch to mind when Pevsner commented on this window. It takes more than a demon to represent the imagery of Bosch but the whole window from which this fragment came must have been superb.

To the east, the capital of the last column is sculpted into stalked trefoil leaves just as you'll see in pocket guides to Gothic architecture. Despite being a regularly used motif they are rare in Surrey. These are even finer than most because they are swept over to the right as though blown by the wind; a beautiful idea that only had a short span of popularity.

Among the memorials don't miss that of 'fryndly Robertt Gardnar' to remind us again of Thorncroft and Elizabeth I. He died in 1571, aged 73. The inscription, more appealing than usual, was composed by her court poet, Thomas Churchyard.

Outside, in the graveyard to the south of the tower is what looks like a pedestal bird bath. It is another one of those drinking fountains provided by the Metropolitan Drinking Fountain and Horse Trough Association but this one is far more ornamental than that at Staines or Woldingham.

From the church the route round to the top of the High Street passes a range of commonplace buildings. This is not to say they don't prompt images of days in their youth when the roads were less busy and the district had its own quiet dignity. This is much more like the Leatherhead known to Jane Austen.

THE HIGH STREET AND SWAN CENTRE
From the Jane Austen part of the town it is only a short walk to the top end of the redesigned part of the town. First the Leatherhead Institute is likely to be spotted as being one of the few 19th century buildings of quality. Dated 1892 it's not a pretentious heap of Victorian self-approval but a solid domestic-looking building with all the conviction of its founder's ideals.

He was a wealthy Birmingham industrialist, Abraham Dixon, who retired to Leatherhead in 1871. Dixon was a great benefactor to the town, apart from founding the Institute for the education and leisure activities of working people (for 2d a week). When it opened, the church bellringers rang 1,893 changes – one for each year of the date.

The Institute stands at the top of a pedestrian precinct which until recently was the High Street. It is now difficult to imagine this thoroughfare choked with traffic. Converting it into a precinct has made a more attractive walkway than is often the case – the scale still feels right, the broken building line now creates character, both along the frontages and the roofline, and efforts have been made to provide a visually varied surface for pedestrians. The intriguing thing is the way it all looks attractive and yet is composed out of little that is individually attractive at all. It does include one early timber-framed building, of great interest to specialists and now happily conserved.

To the west of the High Street were formerly blocks of buildings separated by footways, as indeed still survive in the remaining old parts of the town. These perpetuate the ancient pattern of development, now only really noticeable by the compactness of the present town. All on the west side have been swept away for the Swan Centre, which had its official opening on 8th December 1981. It is low and close with twists and turns, partly open to the air. It has a small enclosing sense of scale, a liberal use of warm brick and a lack of great draughty open spaces. Thus it requires little mental adjustment as you move from the old town into the Centre and back to the town. It works well.

At least it does until it reaches the lower end where the High Street joins the other thoroughfares at what was formerly the ancient and crucial crossroads. The view from here down Bridge Street is now partially interrupted with an incongruous structure like a mini-bandstand. It is debatable whether this townscape view needed punctuating with a tall feature at this point and if it did, it is difficult to believe that this was the most imaginative and worthwhile way of doing so.

The centre here has long been a problem for the planners.

When it was decided to close the Dorking exit to traffic they still had to provide vehicular access to the shops. There was no ideal way of doing so without a bulldozer – and it shows. There's also a flight of wide steps now, from the new down into the old streets, and no wheelchair ramp. Not only is this an offensive denial of rights to the wheelchair user but all the more unbelievable in a town that is proud to serve the nearby Queen Elizabeth Training College for the Disabled.

Earlier this century, redevelopment at the crossroads was more confident. On a corner site a large and boldly assertive building in black and white half-timbering was erected. It is such a feature because there is nothing else like it. Mock Tudor occurs regularly in Surrey and usually of poor design and poor workmanship. This particular building has incurred some rude criticisms which may be unfair. It is too easy to see it as a ghastly imitation, showing little under-standing of its earlier model. If, however, it is accepted as a style in its own right, then it is not nearly so bad. It makes a statement at a focal point, the design is reasonable and the workmanship was better than expended on many of its contemporaries. Certainly Leatherhead wouldn't be the same without it.

Next door is something genuine and good – a cast iron shop front. Feel the fluted columns, smartly painted black and white, and the chill confirms it is not wood. Decorative castings carry a canopy over the pavement, still retaining the bold design. Nearly opposite stands Lloyds Bank, and what an odd design that has. Oh it's all very ordinary at street level but cast your eyes up from this side of the street and the upper levels slope off to one side in a most individual way.

To the left, as the ground rises again, is a genuine piece of half-timbering which the town is proud to have saved. Further up are Jubilee Cottages, another valuable period piece, especially in this corner of the town. Then comes a great surprise – a cottage terrace in local flint. It wouldn't get a second look if it was in one of the nearby villages such as East Horsley or Effingham but it's hardly expected in a main shopping centre.

Beyond, are the council offices, of 1935 and quite a contrast to the waterworks described earlier. There is more ornamentation here, especially if you look closely at the glazing of the cupola. There is still the same emphasis on clean lines though. The cedar tree that once stood in front has now gone but is referred to in earlier guide books as being the last preaching place of John Wesley.

Turning round there is a good view into the dip and up the other side towards the heart of the town. It not only shows well the position of the town on the land's shoulder above the river but is the most visually interesting of the town's views.

Back at the cross-roads, Bridge Street runs down to the aforementioned Running Horse and bridge. As in all Leatherhead's streets there is a wide range of buildings, some showing the presence of the railway by being built of yellow London stock bricks. To take just two for a closer look, try Number 33 with its early 19th century front, punctuated with distinctive pointed windows. It is best appreciated from the other side of the street and then you're on the right side for Coach House Court. This is modern infill which, instead of blocking its site, has been designed to create a sense of space with an entrance-way past one building through to a forecourt of another, set further back. It is all pleasing to the eye and with an intricate small scale appropriate to the town. It's not stark either, for extra money was spent on warm-coloured bricks. They looked just right in the winter sunshine.

Redhill & Reigate

Redhill and Reigate neatly rolls off the tongue and out in the Vale of Holmsdale they merge just as imperceptibly, yet these are no Siamese twins. Redhill is a modern railway town while Reigate is an ancient castle town. Both are rewarding in their own ways.

Lying over the hills that rumple this end of the Vale of Holmsdale, they are backed by the North Downs along which the prehistoric trackway has brought people since earliest times. The Norman invasion force passed this way and in due course the land was portioned out to Richard de Tonbridge, who fortified the ridge to the east, at Bletchingley. He founded the great family of de Clares and as their power increased so the wily King William II tried to balance that power by promoting the de Warennes as Earls of Surrey.

They moved in next to the de Clares and built their castle across the vale at Reigate. Around it developed the present town. The earlier settlement was believed to have been on the opposite ridge where the parish church now stands but there was little proof. Recent excavations, however, have confirmed that this was indeed an early habitation centre. So let's begin at the church.

CHART LANE AND ST MARY'S CHURCH, REIGATE

Today Chart Lane turns off the busy A25 at its junction with the Croydon road and takes a suburban climb up the hillside. Once it was open heathland. That's what 'chart' or 'churt' means – sandy, scrubby heathland – hence the Surrey villages of Limpsfield Chart in the east and Churt in the west.

It has long been conjectured that the hilltop where the church stands was the original settlement, before the present town began developing around the castle walls on the opposite hillside. Recently archaeologists have had the opportunity to confirm that this is indeed an ancient settlement site.

Now only the big medieval church in Perpendicular style reminds us of that. You can wander into the expansive churchyard and into church, right up to the chancel before being hindered by any steps – a rare treat. Inside there's a surprise. The interior was not rebuilt like the outside in the later Middle Ages so the arcades are two centuries earlier, dating from about 1200. During a restoration they were dismantled, but the Victorians admired them so much that they were cleaned and rebuilt, secure for a few hundred years more.

Through in the south chapel there is a modern insertion of interest. It is the glass in the east window for it displays the arms of the six great local families. There you'll see the blue and gold chequers of De Warenne (there is a medieval version in Shere church) together with Elyot, Skinner and Freshfield, Stanley, Cocks and Thurland, Mowbray and Howard. Best known is, arguably, the Howard family, having provided Henry VIII with two queens, Catherine Howard, to whom he was secretly wed at Weybridge, and Anne Boleyn, daughter of Elizabeth Howard, daughter of the Earl of Surrey. Then there's Charles, 2nd Baron Howard of Effingham, who commanded the naval forces against the Spanish Armada and who is buried here.

The Bludders family have their monument here too. Sir Thomas gave 'faithful service to two renowned kings' and his nearby floor slab addresses us in part:

'Reader untill thou knowest how to prize
These neybring Ashes pafse and spare thine eyes.
Ere thou art priviledg'd to weep thou must
Be brought aquainted with this Noble Dust
And know so elegant a worth lyes heer
Twere wrong to staine it with a Common tearc.'

If that makes you smile, see the monument in the north transept to Richard Ladbroke who died in 1730. We are told that he was 'a Zealous Member of the Church' and who could doubt it seeing this monument? There's no Christian humility here! From an artistic viewpoint it is of exceptionally high quality but sadly little is known of its sculptor, Joseph Rose the Elder, except that his skill did not earn him a lasting fortune for he was bankrupt in 1735.

Two other inscriptions might catch the eye. It's not often there is direct reference to murder, but William Burt, army surgeon, was murdered at Godstone on 13th April 1786 – unlucky 13! Then there appears to be a baby wife, for 'Mrs Elizabeth' died aged only 'one yeare and a half old' but that's a trick of our ever-changing language. Here 'Mrs' simply means mistress with no reference to married status. The Henry Hildyard referred to as her father served as an MP and Chamberlain of the Exchequer.

Before you leave, have a look at the font with its wonderful collection of carved heads. It looks very convincingly Perpendicular but it's not really medieval. The Victorians created this. They were having fun with old styles and these faces are indeed fun. The Victorians chose to forget that heads were so rarely carved projecting from the rim because they would displace the natural fall of the decorated font cloth. Such cloths were put out of use at the Reformation and now the design is no hindrance at baptismal services.

For a walk in the town, travel down to the Bell Street car park and the next section.

REIGATE PRIORY AND THE TOWN CENTRE

Ask for the Priory if you get lost and you'll most likely end up in the Bell Street Car Park. Turn your back on the street and walk towards the building in the trees and you'll be approaching the site of the Augustinian priory founded in 1235.

This side is not attractive but skirt round to the left and you'll find colourful rose gardens and a most unexpected landscape. The scene is a secluded vale with extensive grassland sweeping away from the roses, right up to a skyline of woodland. It all runs off to the right until the distant trees close the view. What a surprise next to the town centre!

As for the priory, that was closed down in 1535 by Henry VIII who later, in 1541, granted it to Lord William Howard in exchange for other property. This is the Howard who was raised to the peerage as 1st Baron Howard of Effingham for leading the defense of London during Wyatt's Rebellion. He was the father of the admiral of Armada fame.

No romantic ruins of the medieval priory remain to adorn the park in an 18th century fashion. Instead, there is a grand house with a late Palladian elevation of 1799 fronting the rose garden. The terracotta arms are those of Elizabeth I (added in 1835). It may not be fine enough to get into all the architecture books, but for the general visitor it may be all that the big house in the country park should be.

If time is short it is best spent here but for those with longer a walk back to the car park and left into Bell Street will lead to the town centre.

There is always traffic, keeping the town alive, for Reigate has so far escaped being ripped apart to drive new roads through. Its life is still strung along the streets in a varied medley of building styles going back to Tudor half-timbering. The overall impression is that much of it is from the first 60 years or so of the 20th century so we can still see how the old town was converted to modern needs with dozens of little shops. Such towns are becoming a rarity as more and more are converted again into large-scale centres.

Wedged in among all this is quite a range of older material once you start looking for it. By the car park for instance, is Number 38, a very ordinary 18th century house yet quite noticeable for its honest dignity; nothing pretentious, just solid and reliable and reassuring. Over the road is Number 39, a little more self-assertive yet tastefully restrained. View it from the alley opposite and you can cut out the adjoining buildings, see the evening sun enrich the lovely old brickwork and spot the light rippling back from the hand-made glass in some of the upper windows.

Turn round and continue along the alley to see one of the former commercial sites that helped finance the trading wealth of Reigate which funded such Georgian homes as those just looked at. It is the brewery site with the main building dating from 1786 – see the tell-tale shape of the roof and the word 'ALES' just discernible underneath. The last local brewers were Mellersh and Neale who sold out to the expanding Friary Meux company in 1936. They were based at Guildford, taking part of their name from their site which was formerly that of a medieval friary. Today it has all been replaced by the Friary Shopping Centre. Brewing at Reigate

Reigate brewery

has ceased too. Under Friary Meux the business declined into the making of mineral water, and production finally closed in 1962.

Round past the other associated buildings on the site is a much more emotive relic. A stretch of the old alley still retains its cobbles complete with wagon rails. Get in the right mood and you'll here the shouts of the workmen, the clatter of their clogs and the rattle of the wagons coming down the gradient – imaginary echoes of the days when towns like Reigate had to be largely self-sufficient. (To avoid the cobbles return to Bell Street and so round to the High Street).

The cobbles bring you into the High Street. To the right is

the old town hall (1728) defying the traffic in the former market place. Built to the usual formula, with a ground floor of open arcading to shelter tradesmen and a meeting room up above, it is of brick, the rather dark brick found in this district (and still an important local industry). Architecturally speaking it is said to be the finest building in Reigate but it's not nearly as attractive as some of the homes of the traders who held council here.

From the top of the cobbles turn left, except for the energetic who can now add to this walk by crossing the street and taking the stepped way up between the buildings to climb the castle mound of De Warenne's motte and bailey. In contrast to the formal parkland below the town, this is a wild romantic area of tall grass, trees and native flowers. At the top of the hill is a mock gateway made in 1777 from the last of the castle masonry. A path before it takes you up and over the top of it and then what a surprise you get. Carefully concealed is another park with rose beds and herbaceous borders, (there are level unstepped approaches from the north). This was the focal point of early life in Reigate. This was the objective of the English rebels and the French Dauphin as they tried to crush King John and his supporters (like de Warenne), after John failed to fulfil the promises made in Magna Carta. The castle decided to offer no resistance. Tales still linger, however, despite being disproved, of the rebels plotting Magna Carta in the chalk caverns beneath the castle.

Back in the High Street continue to the west end with its junction with Park Lane and you'll find a building that really is worth seeing. It is the butchers' shop, Marwick and Watson, retaining its original Victorian front complete with colonnaded portico to keep the shoppers dry as they made their choices through the window. The portico is still embellished with its cast iron cresting, bought by the builder from a catalogue in the early days of component mass production. The traffic has tried to demolish the colonnade several times so this rare survival is all the more remarkable.

Diagonally over the junction the range of jettied timber-framed buildings begins Slipshoe Street. They look rather self-conscious here today. With greater naturalness Old

Sweep's House is tucked in behind the far end with many a tell-tale sign of it being just as old under its later cladding. Walk on down to the main road and back up West Street to the Victorian shop and there's a pleasing range of town houses with peeps into little streets designed for horses, all reminding us of the middle classes who played their part in this small market town.

The Coleman family of mustard and orchid fame drove through in their carriage and men touched their caps and the women dutifully cast their eyes downwards. *The Reigate Squires* flowed from the pen of Sir Arthur Conan Doyle while Harrison Ainsworth wrote his last twelve novels from Reigate. George Eliot came into town between writing *Daniel Deronda* out at Earlswood.

Less well known are the books of Eleanor Sinclair Rohde who spent much of her life in Reigate. She was a plant enthusiast and important pioneer in modern herb gardening. Here in her garden at Cranham Lodge she perpetuated rare vegetables and brought forgotten herbs back into use, providing seeds for collectors and knowledge for everyone through her researches and writings.

Back on the walk, from the Victorian shop follow Park Lane down the gradient, past some more attractive houses. Geranium Cottage is particularly eye-catching. To the left is the Priory Park – the bottom end from when it was viewed from the house – so there is a spacious walk back to the car park. It is far removed from the medieval days when this gap or gate in the hills was the hunting place for the roe or reye deer that gave rise to the name of the town.

LOOKING FOR THE EARLY RAILWAY STORIES

Capture Victorian life again outside Reigate Station in Holmsdale Road, where a section of old cobbles still ramps you up to the entrance. Imagine the clatter of the carriage and the jingle of the harness, picture the travellers stepping down at the doorway and see, even today, the projecting columned porch to shield them from the rain. Long may this little gem survive.

It is part of a railway story so important that it gave birth to the great bustling centre of Redhill – Surrey's only other railway town after Woking. Both Redhill and Woking started with nothing, both grew and attracted great institutions, both have been drastically remodelled and both continue into the future as major commercial and commuter centres. So many railway lines and companies come into the story of Redhill junction that it's particularly complicated to disentangle; a job for long winter's evenings rather than this selective poke around the district.

Imagine though, the impact of some 6,000 navvies, mostly Irish, digging their cuttings and tunnels through the hills into Reigate's quiet vale. It must have been good news for Reigate brewery when pay-day came and that lot wanted a drink. It wasn't such good news for anyone caught up in the drunken behaviour and there was plenty of that! Different images come to mind at the thought of the extra 900 horses that came into the district. This was all in the late 1830s when there were food shortages, running up to the Hungry Forties.

How the locals must have been intrigued as workmen began building a tower right on the top of Redhill Common, far from the route of the railway. It was to enable the surveyors to ascertain the correct alignment for the major task of boring the Merstham Tunnel through the hills to the north. The base of the tower is still there and so is the Merstham Tunnel – a great feat of engineering for they ran into no end of troubles. They drove into long-forgotten workings of the ancient stone quarries in the hills, releasing water, causing accidents and fatalities, as though runaway barrows plunging down the cuttings weren't bad enough already.

Services started running (as far as Haywards Heath) on 21st September 1841, with a station at the south end of Hooley Lane (scant remains) known as Redhill and Reigate Roads or simply Reigate. There was still no significant town of Redhill to give its name to the station. Then the following May saw the opening of a branch to Tonbridge with a station at the other end of Hooley Lane and that too was called Reigate. With a line opening to Ashford and its railway works in 1842 the lines began to get busy but the existing arrangement was inconvenient. Another station was built, at the site of the junction, the site of the present Redhill station.

At the time it was of course called Reigate. Life was easier now that the other two Reigates could be closed down.

Attention turned to a line westwards to Guildford and on to Reading to connect with the Great Western services. This opened in 1849 and passed through the town of Reigate behind the castle and so another Reigate station opened – the one in Holmsdale Road. Now at last Redhill came into being to distinguish between them. Redhill station was rebuilt in 1858 but explorers will find parts surviving today.

The Reading/Tonbridge line was not the last local railway venture but it has always been considered vitally important for being the only one to run east-west. That strategic importance was well tested in the Second World War; at the time of Dunkirk 565 trains are said to have passed through Redhill. It was a far cry from when the first line came through and was only provided with First Class carriages, to deter any riff-raff from taking a quick trip to the seaside. Once again the railway company hadn't thought things through and quickly discovered the unpopularity of this arrangement; no one wanted to travel in the same carriage as their servants! Second Class carriages had to be added. It took some time for Third Class travel to be allowed, originally in open trucks, until 1845 when Parliament decreed that all must be covered.

EARLSWOOD AND ST JOHN'S
Redhill begins to make sense as we drive out towards Earlswood and St John's. The town centre of Redhill, like Woking's, has been drastically remodelled since its early days as a Victorian railway town so that it gives the impression that most of its story has been swept away.

Logically the town centre around the station would have needed rebuilding. The cramped design of a small Victorian country town could hardly persist once Redhill grew so large. As we drive out, however, the picture changes. The residential fringe remains, still perfectly able to function. Indeed the late Victorian and early 20th century housing is much sought after. Even where it has been superseded by more recent building or where large gardens have been infilled, the roads themselves reveal their origins. Narrow, with square corners, and blind junctions, these are roads for horses, slower and more manoeuvrable than today's large motor vehicles. So we can still get something of the feel of the early Redhill.

Furthermore the short roads bearing no relation to the lie of the land, full of challenging hill-starts for today's motorist, indicate piecemeal development rather than a grand scheme. Thus Redhill crept up out of the valley site over the flanks of the surrounding hills; it's all up and down out here.

Two types of early development can be spotted. There are those houses built of local rich golden brown stone with tiles of local clay, looking like old country cottages as indeed was their intention. Then there are 'railway age houses' built of materials brought in by train – Welsh slates for the roofs, London stock brick for the walls etc.

This community had its own station of course – Earlswood. It was built in 1868 on the London/Brighton line but the main building (not fully used today) presents us with a period-piece rebuild of 1905 in cheery red brick. It is quite as homely as the residential community it served; far more so than say Brookwood of the same period. On the corner is The Old Chestnut, so obviously the former station hotel, as indeed it was (built 1878).

Looking up from the station, the view is punctuated by the spire of St John's church – a very satisfying piece of town-scaping in the same way as Weybridge church furnishes its corner site when approached from Chertsey. They are both by the same architect, John Pearson. He was 31 when he built Weybridge church and in his seventies when working at Redhill. He had been through a cold, stark phase in the 1860s (see Titsey), going on to produce fine, nationally important churches at Croydon and Upper Norwood in the 1870s, but not flagging in old age when he took on Truro cathedral. He died in 1897, aged 78, before Truro was completed. In his later works we find a return to a more 'friendly' style as here at Redhill, but step inside and the great stone bows across the nave show him still pressing ahead to express himself in new ways.

The site, up on the hillside, adds a lot. The roads dip down in front of it, thrusting it ever higher above us. We're on the edge of the common cut through with little roads and lanes but nothing like the greens outside Christchurch at Esher. Here it's left a wild wilderness of rank grass, bracken, bushes and trees. Town meets country.

Behind the church all sorts of little cottages snuggle into the hillside but the most striking is the long terrace called Carters Cottages strung broadside across the slope above the school and backed by trees. The wooded landscape is new. Old photographs show the common as largely open space with striking views out over the Weald. No wonder the district attracted artists.

Two of the most important spent the last years of their lives at Redhill. One was the famous Samuel Palmer and the other, now less well known was John Linnell, his father-in-law. Through them we are introduced to another great artist and poet, William Blake. It was Linnell who financed Blake's *The Book of Job,* with its visionary illustrations. Four years later Linnell met Palmer and exhorted him to learn from nature, citing Dürer as the finest master to emulate. This Palmer did, thankful that the advice saved him from 'the pit of modern art'. Lucky it did for the fine perception and visionary expression of Samuel Palmer's work is a significant contribution to British art.

Linnell was well into his fifties before he arrived at Redhill, buying up land in the Redstone district, round the hill from the common, designing his own house and settling there. He eventually died in 1882 aged 90. Palmer had died the year before, a mere 76 years old. He is buried in Reigate churchyard. Linnell Road recalls this association but there is little left of the Redhill they loved – just other evocative names like the Sheepwalk to remind us of the pastoral scenes that they were inspired to immortalise.

MERSTHAM
As Redhill grew so it merged with the ancient village of Merstham now strung along the busy A23, but to capture something of its rural past approach it from junction 8 of the M25. You're immediately signposted off the Downs to cut steeply through the fields and woods into Gatton Bottom with Merstham church at the end.

One glance and you can see that to provide such a fine double-aisled church in the 13th century this village must have been important. The tower rises in four stages to a corbel table; the groupings of three lancets, with central ones blind, is far more 'architectural' than is usual in Surrey. The one at Haslemere is so basic it is difficult to date but then 13th century Haslemere was a mere chapelry of Chiddingfold whereas Merstham was an industrial centre. The hills behind were being quarried for 'Reigate firestone' to build Westminster Palace, Old St Paul's Cathedral, London Bridge and Windsor Castle. I wonder how many early burials here were due to quarrying accidents.

There is much to see. Outside, the great feature is the beautiful trefoil-headed west door, enriched with dog-tooth moulding. There's nothing else like this in Surrey. Even more special perhaps is the survival of the ironwork on the door. The semi-pagan motifs found at Old Woking led on to the style found here with flowing scrollwork ending in elegant dragon heads.

Inside, it's the memorials that are likely to attract most attention, primarily the collection of brasses on the floor, the

The west door at Merstham church showing ornate medieval ironwork

walls and one table tomb. The last, to Isabel James, claims her father was mayor (Maioris) of London. What a boast! He was no more than sheriff!

On the south wall is a rare modern figure brass, showing a soldier in the uniform of the First World War. Beside it are brasses to two children. Little Richard Best shows us how a child was dressed in the 1580s but we don't know how old he was, only that he was baptised in the August before his death. Baby brother Peter beside him had died two years before. He is shown still swathed in his chrisom, neatly pinned, which served as a shroud if a baby died during the first month of life.

Further reminders of the high incidence of infant mortality stand as headstones beside the path from the church to the lych gate. One has as many as six infants on it. Some have distinctive lettering while others are badly weathered, but on that to William Cutts aged 15 months we can still read:

'Here lies a child in this spot of ground
Like a flower in the spring: he was cut down
The earthly flower fade: and die away
But he through Christ will never decay'

Ten and a half years later his mother died aged 34 and lies buried beside him.

Less morbid is the lychgate. It is made out of an old windmill, hence the disused mortices and the central iron pillar. Don't forget to look down – you're standing on the millstones!

Down the road, the turning right on the nasty bend takes you into the famous Quality Street. You'll find this cul-de-sac quite wide, with buildings shouldering each other down both sides. There is room for little front gardens all up the left side then a footway and then grassy verges. There is a whole range of buildings spanning five centuries but all so beautifully maintained they wear their age lightly and have a stage-set quality. In the Old Forge at the top lived Sir Seymour Hicks and his wife Ellaline Teriss who both acted in J M Barrie's play that gave its name to this street as a consequence.

Churchyard monument at Merstham

Staines

If I had to choose just one place from all those explored in this book, to show visitors around, it would be Staines: beginning on the waterfront of Egham Hythe, crossing Staines Bridge into what was formerly Middlesex, round the old quarter to the parish church and back to the market square to skirt round the centre.

Staines is the only Surrey town to have been an important Roman town. There is an impressive model of it in the museum. It was important as a bridge town, with its very name of Pontes meaning bridges. In those days the Thames was wider and shallower, with islands in it which the Romans probably linked with bridges. Perhaps these provided the stones that gave the town its English name, or perhaps Staines comes from the stones of the ruins after the Romans deserted.

It didn't die completely. It developed again as a bridge town and trading centre, the birth-place of linoleum but not, as has been claimed, the place where Sir Walter Raleigh was condemned to death. There's plenty to see, so let's begin at the present bridge.

THE BRIDGE, CHURCH AND CONSERVATION AREA

In 1829 the Duke of Clarence laid the foundation stone for the present bridge, hence Clarence Street nearby. The architect was not, as has been claimed, the John Rennie of Waterloo Bridge fame. He had been dead since 1821. Instead it's the work of his sons, George and John, who both followed in father's footsteps. In 1832 the bridge was ready for its royal opening, by which time the Duke had become King George IV.

Happily this noble three-arched structure is still able to fulfil its role today, although it did have to be widened in 1958. Thousands of vehicles cross it every day to bear round to the right into the modern town centre. That means they miss the old quarter which is left in comparative peace, round to the left, signalled by the golden cockerel on Courage's brewery building.

Once you've gone down Bridge Street and turned left into Church Street you're in a gently curving road, dignified with Georgian architecture. Interest begins immediately, with the oldest of the brewery buildings on the corner and best seen from the Moor Lane side. It is of the early 19th century with a tower-like central section indicating its purpose. The wall-ties through it have elliptical heads rather than the more usual discs or crosses. Each is cast with 'Bryan Corcoran, 31 Mark Lane'.

Before this was built the brewing took place in the house (Number 57). Right from the outset of Staines's industrial development brewing played an important part. Even today its successor on the other side of Church Street belongs to Courage's as one of their administrative centres. The site was remodelled in the 1970s but by that time there was an appreciation of the past and so the brewery tower was retained and you can see how the modern was skilfully slotted into the shell of the old 1903 building. It's quite a landmark with some good-looking ironwork decorating the top. What a pity there's a great sign up there; surely the gleaming golden cockerel says it all and so much better.

Previously this brewery had belonged to H and G Simmonds and before that to the Ashbys. At one time there were 16 Ashby households in the town, for this has been one of the great founding families of modern Staines. Like so many other families successful in commerce, they were Quakers and the fine whitened Georgian house projecting beyond the building line a little further down the street was a meeting place of the Society of Friends. The Quaker burial ground lies behind. Notice that when a front window was blocked the frame was retained and only the glazing panels were filled.

Fortunately the planning authorities have been sufficiently vigilant to ensure that the Georgian charm of this street has not been spoiled by modern infills. Island Close at the bottom is decidedly modern (1979-80). It is out of sight but worth a quick look. Despite the pressure to maximise the limited space it creates an attractive place to live. Thought has been given to the provision of privacy around the front doors and although the front is open-plan it does not create a

Staines 1987

St Mary's parish church, Staines

desolation, especially as plants are being used well to break the lines and give all-year interest.

What a surprise lies opposite! St Mary's parish church sits back on a mound of rough grass, with curling path, table tombs and a bordering of trees like many a country church. It's hardly the scene you would expect in such a big, busy commercial town as Staines.

The old church collapsed and this one was built by John Burgess Watson whose only other work in Surrey seems to be the chancel of South Holmwood church. The foundation stone for this one was laid in 1828 which was not in the best period for church architecture and it shows. Attention is usually diverted to the tower which survives from the old church. It bears an inscription stone stating that it was built by the great Inigo Jones, in 1631. That statement has caused debate for generations but it is now deemed erroneous. There is a connection though. Inigo Jones was Surveyor to the Lord of the Manor, King James I.

The stained glass has some tales to tell. There is a modern window commemorating a story from 1215, when Stephen Langton, Archbishop of Canterbury, consecrated the bishops of St David's and Bangor after the signing of Magna Carta at nearby Runnymede. Then there are three Victorian windows given by Kaiser Wilhelm, heir to the German throne, to commemorate a girl from Staines who grew up to be his children's nanny. Her name was Augusta Byng.

Another interesting character was a coloured boy who was boiled to death in a vat of oil in Duncroft House. Well, that's how the story goes but the fact and fiction concerning Duncroft House is as confusing as its architecture. It is one of the last great houses of Staines but the medieval forerunner has gone to leave a mixture of 16th, 18th and 19th century work. You get a peep of it by leaving the church, following Vicarage Road up to the Wraysbury road which you have to cross and then the lane leads on to Duncroft. Watch out for the ghost though. It was sufficiently restless to give its name to Black Boy Lane which used to run down the side of the town hall where there are now gardens.

Opposite the church is The Bells, formerly just The Bell, perhaps recording the church bell. It is an early 18th century building, not of great architectural merit, but playing a particularly attractive role in the street scene. No doubt it has seen some interesting characters trudge up from the waterside. In later times the backwaters here were used for Edwardian children's regattas. Still on the leisure theme there's the Ashby Recreation Ground beyond. That commemorates John Ashby, the last of the great family, who laid the foundation stone for the new pavilion in 1922. Thereon he is described as D L and J P, but that barely indicates his service to Staines. As a Justice of the Peace for example, he served Middlesex for 35 years and Spelthorne for 20. He was also the local county councillor for 20 years and local councillor for 38 years.

Another stone in the pavilion highlights the aged continuity of so much English practice. It takes us back to the early Middle Ages and the evolving manorial system. The inscription reads, in part: 'This building was erected out of part of a sum of £1200 granted by a Court Leet of Sir Alexander Gibbons, Lord of the Manor, held before Harry Scott Freeman his Steward, on 21st day of April 1922, at which Court the following were duly sworn as the Jury. . .' and twelve names follow.

The Court Leet was a regular event, authorised by Royal charter, for overseeing the good conduct of an area and its people. The Steward was originally all powerful with the right to fine or imprison those whom he judged guilty of misdemeanour, but of course by 1922 most of that power had been eroded away.

The manorial system is also perpetuated by the recreation ground itself, for this land was once part of the commoners' Lammas lands. When the enclosure of the common lands was proposed the people hereabouts resisted, as they did in most places, but here they won the retention of some of their land. Several areas survive today and this is one of them. Near the gate note that the drinking fountain records the previous existence of a splendid eccentric-sounding English institution – The Metropolitan Drinking Fountain and Horse Trough Association. Their provisions can also be found at West Horsley, Woldingham, and Leatherhead.

Still in the recreation ground, you'll find, within the railed

The Bells public house at Staines

off area of the children's play pools, a replica of the London Stone. The original, now in safe keeping, was set up in the 13th century to mark the furthest boundary of the jurisdiction over the river Thames of the Mayors of London, (later Lord Mayors). Thus several of their names are inscribed upon the monument. The pedestal dates from 1781. It lost its purpose in 1857 when the Thames Conservancy was formed and began administering river affairs and one of their markers can be seen along the river front.

Before leaving this quarter look up Moor Lane from the end of Church Street and you'll see a noticeable yellow brick house of 1820 and later. It was, believe it or not, a railway station. Originally it was Moor House which went with a mustard mill built beside it, but attempts to link Staines by rail to West Drayton resulted in it becoming Staines West station after the mill was demolished to make way for the platforms. It opened on 2nd November 1885 and the very last train ran on 24th January 1981. Now there is no track, just a fine building to record one episode in the long and tangled history of Staines as a railway junction.

THE MARKET SQUARE AND RIVERSIDE
From the end of Church Street it's possible to cut through other old streets to the market place, where racks of brightly coloured clothing still flap in the winds off the river. This is not, however, the original market place. That was further along and is now replaced by its modern counterpart – Debenhams store.

The present open market site is relatively new for this was the old bridge head, behind the brick wall at the bottom. Behind the town hall too and what a town hall! Surely this is Surrey's finest. It was built in 1880 in ochre bricks with all its classical detailing picked out in white. It has always reminded me of East Anglia so it was no surprise to be told that the architect was John Johnson, from Chelmsford, who was County Surveyor for Essex and whom Pevsner judged to be 'of some merit'. Certainly he brought the light feel of East Anglia to Staines. It is a beautiful building yet even this was threatened with demolition in the 1970s.

The detailing gives it dignity and a certain richness yet

refrains from ostentation. It must have been thought most appropriate as a mark of civic pride in the thriving commercial centre of its day. Beyond stands the old fire station, now the museum, of the same date and same materials but far more sober. It has more of the decorative coloured panels though. Inside is preserved an astonishing little 18th century fire engine from the days when the brigade was a private affair.

Did you read the time off the town hall clock? If you looked at the face overlooking the square did you notice the numerals are wrong? There's an extra eleven instead of a nine. For a bigger optical surprise, stand back from the Blue Anchor on the corner and look at the windows. Notice anything? Five of the windows are not real at all. They have been blocked and the recess painted to look like windows. Those lace curtains are no more than a painter's deception and very deceptive they are too!

Left of the town hall there's access to the river front through a public garden where Staines celebrated its Jubilee in 1964 with the planting of a tree. It's an unusual tree – a Swamp Cypress, I'm told. It is the second oldest known tree, with fossils said to date back 50 million years and obviously quite a surprise when living specimens were discovered in a remote part of China in 1941. It became available commercially in 1948.

From the garden it's a pleasant walk along the riverside when the sun is shining and there isn't an icy wind off the water. Down by the railway bridge you'll come to Thames Lodge Hotel which has been here since at least the 17th century. Earlier it was called The Woolpack from the days when such a cargo was familiar and important on the Thames barges. It has also been called The Packhorse from when cargoes were unloaded nearby. The bollard for tying up still stands.

Also recalling those days is the pair of white cottages between the hotel and the bridge which are known as 'Hook On – Shoot Off Cottages' from the activities of the bargees at this point. Coming downstream from The Hythe was achieved on the current and here the bargees waited to 'hook on' the towing rope for the horse. The upstream journey required more skill. Horses had to be speeded up along the riverside so that at this point the rope could be hooked off to leave the barge to 'shoot off' against the current under its own momentum to reach The Hythe. That was quite demanding for one horse so an enterprising gentleman took to hiring out a team to do the job. There was so much traffic that this was an economic proposition. The system didn't work at all of course if the barge had to stop at this point. To solve that they simply floated a rope down from The Hythe and then hauled the barge across. The horses were taken by road over the bridge or else were ferried across. Neither practice was of any great age because before the 19th century the barges were powered by men, called bowhaulers, because they hauled on the rope attached to the bow, but in the local speech is was pronounced more like a cricket 'bowler'.

Other problems arose here when the barges found themselves grounded because the millers had taken so much water. The river was wider and shallower then and so a drop in level was all the more noticeable. Yet another problem arose in 1855-6 when the railway bridge was built because its brick abutments promptly started fraying the tow ropes. The solution to that problem can still be seen on the brickwork – rollers. They seem too far back to be necessary but that's an indication of the earlier width of the river. The shallows were reclaimed and the new land bought by public subscription to commemorate Queen Victoria's Jubilee in 1877, as you'll find recorded on the fine old lamp-standard beyond the bridge.

There you'll find reminders of a totally different viewpoint of the Thames – not the working river but the scenic site to develop with river-front villas for the middle classes. Here some still stand, with their smart decorative cast iron balconies and a fashionable smattering of stained glass. When even more land came up for sale as building lots the people protested loudly enough to persuade Sir Edward Clarke, QC to announce that if the people could manage to buy the riverside field then he would build a church on it and save it from housing for ever. Thus St Peter's church was built, in a demure Perpendicular style, looking every bit an early 20th century building. It was in fact consecrated in 1894 when we might expect a last wild fling from the Gothic revival.

From the church you can return along the road to town where the modern Elmsleigh Centre will be ahead of you. It is named after the house that stood here from 1828 onwards. One of its residents was a Dr Tothill, hence the name of the car park.

From the Thames-side area skirt the Elmsleigh Centre towards the north-west corner and the London Road. This short stretch is past the car parks and bus station but the latter is better than some for being long and narrow, following the curve of the road and thus enhancing the townscape. It is a good use of the 'marginal' land until, I suppose, there is more development on this side.

Soon you'll reach the railway bridge where there was once a station but it didn't last long – another link in the tangled history of railways in Staines. Beyond the bridge is the Garibaldi with some old brickwork, reminders of the days when this was part of a row of old cottages at the edge of the town. Beyond it is a parade of shops from the coloured panel-pierced concrete period, grandly called Majestic House but it's not pretension. It records the former existence here of the Majestic Cinema, from 1939-1951. Staines had five cinemas, now only one, believed to be the first multi-screen cinema outside London.

Next of note is the post office in a smart little building of bright red brick with white rustication and a further nod to the classical with its pair of urns enriched with swags on the ends of the roof parapet. Then comes Badgers, dated 1933, with the new proportions and decorations that became popular in the 1930s.

Opposite, the pierced roofline of Central Parade successfully unites a very nondescript row of shop fronts and has now been townscaped well by the new red brick building on the end which carries the eye round the corner. Behind it is more of the same but rising high as Magna House and providing more good townscaping when viewed from the road junction.

Now for a smile. It's the police station in a Victorian house of yellow stock brick built in 1876. The first occupant of the cells was the man who had just finished building them, having got drunk and disorderly on the proceeds! Behind it, London Road continues with Staines Ash Parade which makes an interesting comparison with Central Parade for being a late Victorian solution to the same problem.

Over the road is a most singular piece of modern architecture, now used by British Gas. The main offices are a boring glass box but beside it on the lawn stands an incredible mushroom-like extension. The stair tower spoils the beautiful sense of balance, from some angles, but I presume fire regulations etc determined such an addition. This, and the Thorncroft building at Leatherhead, are the two modern buildings that most held my attention while recording for this book.

Finally, round behind Magna House you'll find the Adult Education Centre, housed in a building known as the Oast House. It was no such thing. It was another brewery, built of slate and yellow stock brick between 1824 and 1851, for the Harris Breweries. They were taken over by Ashbys in 1903. Everywhere you turn there seems to be an Ashby connection and everywhere you turn there is something of interest.

Thames Ditton

Eros was born here! The famous London statue was cast in Burton's brass foundry which, from the 1870s, became Cox and Co. They were famous for their ecclesiastical work and large public monuments such as the Peace memorial on Constitution Arch, London and the Polyapes Scout memorial at Stoke D'Abernon here in Surrey. A royal subject attracted a visit from George V and Queen Mary.

The foundry has closed but a lot else survives at Thames Ditton, cramped along the riverbank trying not to get its feet wet. The Swan is one of the oldest buildings, dating back to the 16th century and then a succession of other buildings from the succeeding centuries, strung along the narrow streets. Most are of red brick but a few are in the local Thames-side style of white weatherboarding. Even the top of the church tower is so treated before it finishes off with a short lead spire.

The churchyard has a wide variety of memorials, including some broken pieces from the 1870 bombing of Monmartre in Paris. They commemorate Pamela Fitzgerald, daughter of the Duke of Orleans and half sister of Louis Philippe, exiled to Claremont at nearby Esher, during the Revolution. She had been at the court of Marie-Antoinette and died in 1831.

The church is worth a visit. Inside there is much to see and much of it well recorded. Surprisingly, one national rarity is given scant attention. It is the set of paintings of wooden panels over the chancel arch, dating from about 1570. The set is no longer complete but there's enough to give a good impression of the arrangement in pre-Reformation days when such Doom paintings were a familiar backdrop to the great rood or crucifix placed in front. This arrangement was the focal point in the church, not the high altar of today. Each Doom gave a dire warning about the Day of Judgment, until their universal destruction was ordered by law during the Reformation and so few pieces survive today.

Have a look at the font too. It is the only Norman font in Surrey with figurative sculpture. It's not a great masterpiece like Eardisley in Herefordshire but nevertheless in its own simpler way shows us motifs not so easy to find elsewhere. The most important is the Agnus Dei or lamb holding a cross with a flag. This represents Christ and is one of the oldest Christian symbols, occurring in the frescoes of the catacombs. Very often it is accompanied by strange beasts as a reminder that all powers are brought to peace through Christ. Here at Thames Ditton is one so rare that it is not often recognised for what it is. The 'goat' standing on its head is an ibex plunging downwards, illustrating the belief that its horns were strong enough to save the creature from any fall because they represented the Old and New Testaments.

Outside, interesting buildings are scattered around the village. For a different style of church there is the United Reformed church. Mrs H Wilfred Scriven of Tudor Court, Cobham, laid the foundation stone in 1899. The architect, W H Woodroffe, took trouble with it, creating a happy blend of detail with scale although the dormer windows could be improved. The octagonal bell turret tapering to a smart copper roof is particularly distinctive.

Other examples show how the Victorians took a simple village and built up its resources to serve the needs of the expanding community. A cottage hospital was provided and that still stands. Then it was time to celebrate Queen Victoria's Diamond Jubilee and for this the lord of the manor of Weston, Hannibal Speer, paid for a village hall, 'for the perpetual use and enjoyment of the parishioners'.

Earlier provisions are represented by the almshouses for six men and women of the parish in accordance with the will of Henry Bridges in 1720. These then, are notable for being such an early survival of Georgian architecture in the county. Henry Bridges was the local Justice of the Peace and styled Lord of the Manor of Imber Court. In the wall of his building three stones record restorations but note in particular that the original sundial, dated 1720, is still in situ, inscribed 'vigilate & orate.'

Walton church

Walton on Thames

The town centre of Walton on Thames is still fairly small, despite its proximity to London and having a main line station. The proximity of other towns has no doubt limited its development by dispersal while in earlier times the unbridged Thames cut it off from all its neighbours beyond.

It escaped having its church rebuilt or heavily Victorianised and so we can still walk into this historic heart and admire the Norman arcades in the nave. A fine building, it has a lot of interest.

A couple of its tales seem unbelievable today. One arises from an inscription on the wall which says:

'Christ was the worde and spake it
He took the bread and break it
And what the worde doth make it
That I believe and take it.'

This testament of faith in the Holy Communion service is attributed to none other than Queen Elizabeth herself. At least, that is the tradition but I'm not the first to doubt it! I can't imagine Her Majesty exerting so much effort to return the country to Protestantism after lapsing into Catholicism under Queen Mary, to then express her boredom with the church service by indelibly scratching messages into the church wall, with everybody watching. However, I can imagine one of her ladies in waiting or other attendants becoming so bored with the repetitious homages to Her Majesty that the carving exercise provided most welcome relief.

Royal visits arose from the Palace of Oatlands lying between this town and neighbouring Weybridge. Elizabeth's keeper of the park was one John Selwyn and it is his memorial here in Walton church that provides the other curious tale. One of the constituent brass plates shows John riding astride a stag while at the same time stabbing it through the throat. During this improbable feat he is shown keeping his hat smartly in place.

The explanation as worded in the 1807 *Antiquarian Repertory* says Selwyn 'in the heat of the chace, suddenly leaped from his horse upon the back of the stag (both running at that time with their utmost speed) and not only kept his seat gracefully, in spite of every effort of the affrighted beast, but, drawing his sword, with it guided him towards the Queen, and coming near her presence, plunged it into his throat, so that the animal fell dead at her feet.'

One would have thought that to deliberately guide a charging stag straight at Queen Elizabeth would have put him in the Tower. Indeed an alternative story is more easily accepted – that the usual spectacle of driving a fine stag along a marked route past the queen went wrong. The stag deviated off course, straight towards Her Majesty, until Selwyn sprang upon it and killed it in the nick of time.

It was obviously a moment to be proud of and trouble was taken to record it so graphically on the brass, for you'll find it's a palimpsest (ie it is engraved on both sides). The back shows another version of the same scene but only lightly engraved. Presumably the artist put forward at least these two versions for final approval. We can see why this one was rejected. It is far less dramatic and, horror of horrors, he hasn't got his hat on! In the presence of the queen without his hat on! Oh dear, what were manners coming to?

That wasn't the only mistake the poor artist made. He misspelled keeper as kepper in the inscription and we can still see where he altered it. He also missed the 'o' out of 'sons' but he seems to have got away with that as an abbreviation.

Outside the church there is much less of interest in the town itself, unless you swallow any prejudice against modern developments and look at the style of what has been done. It is of interest because it dates from the early 1960s and is thus one of the first schemes in Surrey in the new style. The shopping centre was sufficiently ready for an official opening by Honor Blackman in 1965 followed by Princess Margaret's opening of the new town hall the next year.

Compared with former landscapes there is a new emphasis on space, with the wide road curving out of the centre towards the bridge. The shops on the left are set back with a pedestrian way branching off at an angle. Over the road short tower blocks of flats stand boldly in grassy lawns. It all sounds good but always leaves one rather disappointed. Instead of the ideas coming together to form a fresh townscape they seem to spread so far out that they no longer relate to each other.

New Zealand Avenue along the back is very boring except the unexpected name. It commemorates New Zealand soldiers given medical treatment in the town during the First World War. There were two hospitals serving them. One was Oatlands Lodge towards Weybridge and the other was Mount Felix near the bridge end of the Avenue. Look across the road and you'll spot its cedar trees and an orange-brown tower.

The italian-looking tower is by Sir Charles Barry, of Houses of Parliament fame, from his remodelling of an earlier house for the 5th Earl of Tankerville. It was quite a house in those days. What caught the attention of the Duke of Devonshire was the palm tree in the 'incomparable' palm house. The Duke was having his own grand (and now famous) conservatory built at Chatsworth and that palm was just what he wanted. Lady Tankerville let him have it too.

The tree was 50ft high and 8ft 4in round, weighing about 12 tons. It took eleven horses to draw the specially built wagon but off it went in early September, 1840. There were frequent delays along the 180 mile journey while toll gates were dismantled to let the great load through. It got there even if the journey did cost the Duke about £1,000 for the pride of owning the finest palm tree in the land.

In comparison, how humble is the little pansy. Pansies became an interest of the gardener at Mount Felix, a Mr Richardson, at the beginning of the 19th century. Far from being commonplace they were new exciting garden plants recently created by hybridising the little wild species of pansy. He introduced a new blue strain from the Continent and also fired the enthusiasm of the Earl's youngest daughter, Lady Mary Bennet. She was soon growing them herself in her own flower beds so that Mount Felix was able to claim the first and finest collection in the kingdom.

Nurseryman James Lee of Hammersmith lured Richardson

Victorian terracing at Walton on Thames

away to breed new strains. By 1814 they had created about 20 new varieties. These became the basis for the strains we grow today. Their popularity was instant, especially with the poor in industrial areas. In 1899 James Simkins wrote of the pansy: 'it is inexpensive, it is easily managed and it is beautiful, and beauty is a thing more needed by the poor than the rich.'

Beyond Mount Felix lies that part of the Thames known as Cowey Sale, with its odd story of a bridge that changed the county boundary. There was no bridge at all until 1750, to join Surrey with the former Middlesex. That first bridge was of a very striking design, perhaps by William Etheridge, with masonry ends and piers but with the central section of geometric open woodwork in the fashionable Chinese style – so striking that the great artist Canaletto painted it not once but twice. It didn't last long and its successor was the one recorded by another great artist, J M W Turner.

It was the third bridge that caused the boundary fuss. When it fell into disrepair the Middlesex authorities did nothing about it, although it was their bridge, for the county boundary ran along the Surrey bank. The Surrey people were enjoying the increased trade that the bridge had brought and so the magistrates charged Middlesex with responsibility for repairing it. Middlesex denied responsibility. Surrey brought a criminal action for neglect. That was unsuccessful because it came to light that all the judges involved came from Middlesex! Into the story comes the county of Kent, where the Maidstone Assizes heard the case before a special jury in July 1877. What a sitting that must have been! All the carefully prepared arguments were to no avail. The jury said simply that when it came to bridging two counties the boundary was best thought of as running down midstream. Each county should repair its own half. Accordingly the boundary was moved out to midstream.

That iron bridge of 1863 continued to cause problems, having been damaged in the Second World War and declared unsafe in 1953. The 'temporary' replacement is still in use, causing such a notable bottle neck that once again a new bridge is being promised. This time though it will be all Surrey's since the county boundary has been changed again!

Cowey Sale is an attractive grassy terrace beside the river, very popular with ducks and geese and on sunny afternoons, with people. Its odd name of Sale probably comes from 'salh', the Anglo Saxon for willow (hence sallow for pussy-willow) from when great willow beds grew all along the Thames here and up to Staines, fostering one of the country's five great basket-making centres.

Of course the usual story that has been told here is that Julius Caesar took the Roman legions over the ford. The old wooden ford markers were pointed out to prove it. One authority even assured readers that the stakes were of yew wood – very significant and about as probable as Queen Elizabeth carving up the church during Holy Communion!

Weybridge

Weybridge is still surprisingly small for such a well known place. The fame began right back in the 16th century when Henry VIII had a palace built here at Oatlands and started to attract outsiders to a tiny village at the confluence of the river Wey and the Thames. In due course other country houses were built adjacent to the village street, owned by dukes and admirals and earls. One had even been given by King James II to his mistress, Catherine Sedley. It was the visitors they attracted, or the notoriety that deterred them, that maintained the name of Weybridge, long after the royal palace had been demolished during the Civil War period. Thus the village had several important households adjacent to its centre, rather than the usual story of one 'big house', the Manor. Sadly none of these has survived today.

It wasn't until the railway age that the village really began to grow into a town, so let's begin at the station, out on the Byfleet road.

THE RAILWAY STATION DOWN TO THE TOWN

At the railway bridge the most surprising sight is not a town but the lack of one. The view is almost entirely of trees, but the woodland floor is carpeted with ivy – a sure indication that this woodland is of no great age. Indeed the last few gorse bushes are still struggling for the light, showing this to have been open heathland. We must imagine the early travellers arriving on this ridge amid beautiful open countryside with wide views over Surrey and that is indeed how it has been recorded in the writings of many of the famous visitors. That's why they came.

One was Robert Louis Stevenson who stayed in the Hand and Spear Hotel across the back of the station car park. There he worked on *Treasure Island* (published 1882) and his desk may be seen in Weybridge Museum.

Beyond the car park is Brooklands Technical College holding the key to the lack of development. The heathland, being rather unproductive, was gathered with other lands to form an estate around a large house, acquired in 1830 by Peter King, 7th Baron King of Ockham. He died in 1833 so it was his son, the Honourable Peter King who had the house here at Brooklands rebuilt (the nucleus of today's college) and this is the King who saw the coming of the railway.

From the station bridge the most noticeable feature is the deep cutting for the track. It's something expected of railways and so obscures our appreciation of the immense effort exerted by the teams of navvies to create it. It was, after all, dug by hand and even in its day the cost caused concern. It was the first main railway line in Surrey, the first part of a great network that in one generation would transform a countryside that had been shaped by thousands of generations.

The opening date, 1838, can be seen on the keystone of the restaurant entrance on the end of the bridge. This was the first station until the present one was opened in 1902. The old one is the best surviving piece of railway architecture from this first phase. In 1863 part of it became the post office but go down the hill towards the town and you'll find another, The Old Post House, on the corner of Elgin Road. It's quite a fun building, playing with the potential of brick to create architectural detailing and ornament. Along Elgin Road itself lived the landscape artist T H Maclachlan (died 1897).

Still passing through the wooded estate the road now reaches a green: a most attractive approach to the town. On the right is the Roman Catholic church of St Charles Borromeo built in 1881 and opened by Cardinal Manning. It retains its tiny predecessor, built as a private family chapel in 1835 by local landowner James Taylor, and this chapel has some tales to tell.

On 7th March 1848 the former king and queen of France attended mass here. Louis Philippe had abdicated in February and turned to the English royal family for help and had been given a safe refuge at Claremont, Esher. They were unable to celebrate the Roman Catholic Mass, however, because the estate was Crown property and Queen Victoria was head of the Anglican Church.

Weybridge wasn't a long coach ride away and so began its long association with the Royal House of Orleans, involving

Weybridge church

the burial of 13 of its members in the vault beneath the little chapel. All except the Duchess of Nemours, cousin to both Queen Victoria and Prince Albert, have now been returned to France, to their family mausoleum at Dreux in Normandy, following changes in French law.

Those readers who would like to continue this semi-rural walk before entering the town can take the lane that runs along the bottom of the green. Among the variety of houses the most interesting is Eastlands, hiding behind garden walls. It features in the childhood memories of the actress Fanny Kemble (died 1893), daughter of actor Charles Kemble and niece of Sarah Kemble, better known as the actress Mrs Siddons. Her father remained during the week in their London home at 5, Soho Square. Only for weekends did he make the two or three hour coach ride to Weybridge: 'a rural, rather deserted-looking, and most picturesque village'. Thus it is mother who features most strongly in the witty memoirs, with her 'perfect passion for fishing'. She 'was perfectly unobservant of all rules of angling' so they had some glorious carefree days on the banks of the river Wey, no doubt frowned upon by the London society of the 1820s as being, well, rather quaint.

Fanny thought the Wey 'made it a place an artist would have delighted to spend his hours in'. Little did she know that a notable Royal Academician would live in her very childhood home. He was Edward Millington Synge, a land agent for the Locke-King estates. After the First World War the novelist Warwick Deeping lived here, until his death in 1930. It is not open to the public.

Further on is the modern county council architecture of Heathside School. Having three storeys it absorbs less room and in fact manages to hide quite discreetly among all the trees on the site. It must be the most unobtrusive state school of its date in the county.

The lane continues round the hill and ends at Brooklands Farm with fields of red deer for venison farming. Nearby is Laundry Cottage, reminding us of the do-it-yourself days on large estates like Brooklands, for the lane has brought us round the hill to a point below the house. The water meadows of the river Wey lie all round but there are no

View of Weybridge

public footpaths, so explorers must retrace their steps back to the green and turn left for the town.

ALONG THE TOWPATH
As you reach the edge of the town from the station, Bridge Road can be followed along to the left, to the river. Here prehistoric peoples forded the Wey and lost their flint tools, now displayed in the museum. By early medieval times there was a bridge that gave its name to the adjoining settlement on the river terrace cut into the low hills between the Wey and the Mole.

Bridges here were of wood, right up to the factory age and the provision of the fine cast iron product of 1865 that is still in use today. At the far end the canalised section of the Wey Navigation (opened 1653) sneaks in to rejoin the river and swirl its waters into the great pool that was once the 'port' of Weybridge. Barges from London docks could swing round here to tie up at the wharf still standing on the far side. Others were hauled or poled past to continue inland to Guildford. After 1764 they could reach as far as Godalming.

Manoeuvring barges round the corner from the pool into the canal was tricky. The solution was to provide the post on the corner to guide the tow-ropes round, It's still there, complete with vertical roller to prevent the ropes fraying on the post.

By walking round the back of the buildings you can reach the towpath and follow it downstream – a surprisingly rural walk lined with trees making it difficult to believe Weybridge High Street is just over on your right. Up ahead lies the last lock before the Thames with its attractive lock keeper's cottage. When that was found to be beyond repair, The National Trust, who own the Wey Navigation, decided to rebuild it to look the same as it did before, so this corner seems to have changed very little for decades.

The adjoining mill stands on an island created at the time of the Navigation by providing an overflow channel. By 1693 a Robert Douglas had built a paper-making mill here but that growth industry was soon over-exploited and by 1720 it was more profitable to hammer out iron with hundreds of hoops needed for the local barrel-making industry exploiting Surrey's oak woods. After the Napoleonic Wars demand fell, a general depression set in and the mill was vacated and neglected. Villagers stripped it of valued materials while years of litigation rambled on. By 1842 when Thomas Metcalf Flockton leased the site the mill was in ruins but he rebuilt it for crushing oil-seed and it was while leased out for this purpose that it suffered one of its most spectacular fires.

Barrels of oil waiting on the wharf for despatch were rolled into the lock for safety while fire swept through the refining sheds. Great vats of oil in there burst and sent 'a real stream of fire' running out and into the lock where it set off the barrels. 'The scene was now awfully grand. Flames rose from the water higher than the fourth storey of the mill' reported the fire officer with more than a little enthusiasm. Braving the flames, someone thought to open the lock gates and flush all the problem out into the Thames – where lots of moored boats were in the way! That's how Weybridge celebrated Christmas Eve and the early hours of Christmas Day in 1877!

The other side of the island is reached simply by following the path, over a driveway and straight ahead into Church Walk. This is Weybridge's most delightful of 19th century housing, all tucked in together. The yellow London brick and

Radnor Road, Weybridge

blue Welsh slates demonstrate wider markets and improved transport systems. Turn left and you can make your own way out to the Thames and follow another tow-path up to Walton. Turn right and you can walk through the back streets to Weybridge town centre.

Most of the main shopping street was rebuilt in the early decades of the 20th century and has little more than that to interest the outsider. It is becoming increasingly interesting for just that though, as other towns get ripped apart for new road schemes and shopping facilities get grouped under roofs, and traffic excluded from pedestrian-only streets. Here, the shop-lined thoroughfares that were the Weybridge known far and wide, still survive.

Woking

In 1988 Woking celebrated its 150th birthday and much was made of the founding and development of this important railway town, and doesn't need repeating. There's more to Woking than railways though. In 1990 the original settlement, now called Old Woking, celebrated 900 years of existence, centered upon its church of St Peter – a popular dedication for churches remote in the countryside.

OLD WOKING

The long straggling street still follows the ancient settlement line. Behind it rose the heath-covered upland upon which the railway town was built. Below it were the wetlands of the Wey Valley, soon cleared of willows and alders to make the water meadows that remain today, still carved through with watercourses. On a spur of drier land running into the

Viking Saga door at Old Woking

meadows the church was built. Notions that it was once a monastery are erroneous, arising from a misunderstanding of the term minster.

The new Christian world arrived and displaced the pagan, represented symbolically, it seems, in the ironwork of the west door of the church in the late 11th century. Probably taking its motifs from the Viking *Voluspa* poem, it reminded people of 'Ragnarok', the End of the World.

The great serpent Jormungand rose to overwhelm the world with its evil, shown top right of the door, looped over a swastika, the symbol of Thor the High Thunderer, who led the attack against it and failed. Surt, the Fire God, fell too, shown as the spiky loop, his sun disc symbol, falling to a spiky horizontal bar - perhaps the oars of one of the ships featured in the poem - Naglfar, made of dead men's nails that the giants rose in, or the ship that the Evil Loki sailed with the inmates of Hell. Defiant at the top stands the Christian cross, a new symbol of salvation for all who pass beneath it into the protection of the Church.

Centuries later the balance of power was rocked in a different way. Edmund Beaufort, 2nd Duke of Somerset and Lord of the Manor of Woking, was considered the most likely person to attract the marital intentions of Henry V's young widow, Catharine of Valois. It was the first time an English king's widow had not returned to her homeland and we weren't sure what to do about it. One chronicler pointed out that she `was unable to curb her carnal passions', so she would be looking for a new husband. Royal blood didn't run in any suitable veins so the awful truth dawned that she might marry one of the king's subjects and thereby allow a commoner to influence the upbringing of Catharine's son, the king.

The two most powerful men in the country were the Bishop of Winchester and the Duke of Gloucester. The former was Edmund's Uncle Henry and so he was quite happy for a royal marriage in the family. Humphrey, Duke of Gloucester, was not.

While Edmund was safely out of the way campaigning in France, Gloucester introduced legislation that made such a marriage punishable by the bridegroom losing his estate for

Church approach, Old Woking

life, thus preventing him from supporting the royal family. Furthermore, the dowager queen must have the king's consent for such a marriage and the king must be of age to give it. Catharine's son, Henry VI, was only six so Gloucester hoped he had the situation under control for a good few years yet.

Catherine had other ideas. She got married secretly, not to Edmund but to Owen Tudor and in due course the Duke of Gloucester's fears were fulfilled, when a certain Henry Tudor won the battle of Bosworth and took the crown of England. His mother was Margaret Beaufort, Lady of the Manor of Woking.

The rise and fall of the manor and palace, its pillaging to build Hoe Place and local farms, together with the stories of the replacement Manor House in the village centre have all been much repeated.

Less well known is the argument between the vicar and a local householder over the proposal to install a clock in the church tower. The vicar won so the householder blocked his own view of it by building a high house beside the churchyard at the lych-gate! Stand back in the churchyard and you can read the date set with different coloured tiles in the roof.

This churchyard cul-de-sac with some medieval buildings is the best bit of Old Woking but move back along the street and there's a refurbished terrace that shows so clearly how well old properties can be renovated to modern standards without destroying our heritage. Then, at the road junction there's the old brewery in Georgian red brick beside the post office. Four breweries once served the borough; two have gone completely, one partly survives as outbuildings, but there's plenty to see of this one.

Opposite is the later manor house with distinctive dutch gables. Built of two stages, it has been suggested that the oldest is from 1620 when James I gave the royal manor to Sir Edward Zouch. The architecture, however, cannot be before 1650 and is more likely to be from the 1660s when the royal manor was to revert to the crown. The right-hand larger portion dates from about 1680.

Further along the street a detour can be made up the lane

The Old Manor House, Old Woking

to see the impressive watermill of Unwin Brothers' printing works. The company built it early this century so as to move out of their previous works at Chilworth. There they had been sharing the waters of the Tillingbourne with gunpowder makers but found that explosions filling the air with burning debris were not compatible with paper making!

Further along the main street there is a timber-framed farmhouse reminding us of the rise of the yeoman as the Tudor enclosures ended open field agriculture and fostered the development of small farmsteads. The days of the great fields were over. Here, the Broadmead survives but the other two have been built on and given their names to the new districts of Kingfield and Westfield.

The daughter church of St Mark at Westfield looks rather domesticated. That's because it was built originally as the school. When a second school was built opposite, the original became the church.

WOKING TOWN

At the time of writing, Woking town centre was being rebuilt for the second time, but something of its beginnings can be discovered behind the station.

Behind the station means the opposite side to the town centre but it was in fact designed as the front! It leads out into residential areas, winding surburban roads with grass verges, street trees, detached houses and mature gardens etc. It's hardly everyone's idea of a modern town centre, even with its recent infills, let alone a railway town but that's all part of why Woking is the third most expensive place to live in the country. Explore on up to the highest ground and you'll reach even more impressive high status areas. The Hockering is a fine example of planned development – large detached houses with large gardens laid out as a private estate now rich with mature trees and beautifully maintained. It's the outsiders' stereotyped notion of Surrey but of which the county has so few examples.

Alternatively, bear left out of the station forecourt and walk along Oriental Road. At the end follow the factory of James Walker and Co Ltd, downhill to Gate No. 1. You can't go in but you can see, set back, the red-brick Victorian building with hints of grandeur. This was the Royal Dramatic College.

The college arose from a meeting back in July 1858 between Charles Dickens and William Thackeray, who were concerned about the plight of the acting profession. Thus this was not a college for drama students but for those too old or ill to work – 'decayed' as *The Times* called them. The royal part was played in 1860 when the foundation stone was laid by the Prince of Wales. This was Albert, Prince Consort, and not the future Edward VII as sometimes claimed.

Superb illustrations survive, showing a vast range with central tower, to match the idealism of the cause. Alas, the cause foundered and the building was sold off in 1880. The base of the tower and four bays each side survive and are what we look along from the viewpoint out in the street. The top of the tower proved weak and has been removed. Also missing are the end bays and the cross wings of the early illustrations but it is now doubted whether they were ever built. They do not appear in any of the early photographs.

The illustrations could well have been based on the architect's drawings as the great building must have been under scaffolding for several years as extension followed extension. This might explain why the inscribed foundation stones do not always concur with documentary evidence.

Inside, but not open to the public, is the great hall where such famous actors as Sir Henry Irving performed to the 'annuitants', the first of whom took up residence on 29th September 1862. It was then open up to its fine timbered roof (medieval style) but has, at some unknown date, been floored across. That brings anyone in the upstairs chamber within close viewing distance of the stained glass (unsigned) in the two great rose windows. That in one gable shows ten scenes from Shakespeare's comedies and the other from his tragedies.

This impressive room is now beautifully maintained as the board room of James Walker & Co Ltd.

Enjoying a drive into Surrey out of London's East End one weekend in 1926 was a certain George Cook. He had begun a career in manufacturing at 16, working for James Walker. It was he who promoted their engineering products into world leadership and it was here he chanced upon the large site their expanding enterprise needed so much. At first it seemed too big but by wisely anticipating future needs and outstripping competitors with their quality, the company soon filled the site. Even with all the latest labour-saving technology they are still the largest employer in the borough, ensuring they live up to their trade mark, the lion – the king of beasts for the king of products.

Originally, the company concentrated upon all sorts of fluid seals for the ever increasing power of new engines and machines – 'there were few major ports where the man from James Walker was not a regular visitor, calling on vessels from many nations'. Now they have companies in nine of those nations and still have agents wherever their products could serve.

Returning to Oriental days, turn off Oriental Road down the side of the Lion Works and you'll find a mosque set in grassland with trees. Its full name is the Begum Shah Jehan Mosque after the queen of Bhopal in the 1860s.

Ruins of Newark Priory, Woking

It's a striking little building in blue and white, duly orientated towards Mecca by one of P & O's captains who came to Woking to take the bearings. All was not so simple though for the architect, W I Chambers, who fell out with Dr Leitner and someone else finished it off. Their differences wrangled through the print of *Building News* until the editor was provoked into wishing 'the Mosque at Woking had been built at Jericho or some place distant enough never to have troubled us'. It was the first mosque to be built in Britain and one of the few named after a woman.

Walk on downhill from James Walker's Gate No 1 and under the railway bridge you can turn left into Maybury Road. Here the writer H G Wells came to live in 1895. He borrowed £100 and 'furnished a small, resolute, semi-detached villa with a minute greenhouse in the Maybury Road facing the railway line where all night long the goods trains shunted and bumped and clattered – without serious effect upon our healthy slumbers'.

He set about writing *The War of the Worlds* which contains vivid impressions of the early Woking and its neighbour-hood. It is especially interesting because he didn't change the place names so we can relocate the scenes exactly.

It's not surprising that he remembered the minute greenhouse because here he began his enthusiasm for gardening and illustrated his diary with a cartoon of himself bearing his first harvest – a marrow. Plenty of others were taking a keen interest in gardening too because the great heathlands were undeveloped and suitable for nursery fields. Two of the country's great nurserymen worked their fields here – Waterer and Jackman. Soon this whole area was given over to nursery fields of world importance: a story researched and published by E J Willson as *Nurserymen to the World*. Now their lands have been largely built over. Goldsworth Park was claimed to be the largest private housing estate in Europe. Knaphill and St Johns are older.

KNAPHILL
Squidged in between Brookwood, St Johns and Goldsworth Park, it is never very clear which is which, except that the centre of Knaphill is on top of Anchor Hill and that the centre is not worth looking at.

Down the hill there's a country-looking pub to remind us of the days before modern development, and a walk over the corner of the green to go up Barrs Lane leads out into fields and lanes still hedged with hazel. At the beginning of Barrs Lane there are two very fine groups of rosy-red buildings going back to the 16th century and always eye-catching when the sun is on them.

Knaphill has been known for its brickmaking which began in the 1790s for the construction of the Basingstoke Canal. Later, thousands of bricks were needed for the great Victorian enterprises of Brookwood Hospital for the mentally ill and the prisons. Both men and women were imprisoned here but the prison was only used for about 30 years. In 1895 the men's prison was converted into Inkerman Barracks and four years later the women's was added to it. In 1965 it closed but is still remembered by Inkerman Road, Inkerman Way and Barrack Path. The brickworks on Anchor Hill closed in 1925.

ST JOHNS

Here you can escape modern developments to walk the towpath of the Basingstoke Canal or the grass and woodland of the Lye. The latter is due to the efforts of the Rev Charles Bradshaw Bowles, vicar of Woking back in 1854. He saw the London Necropolis and National Mausoleum Company buying up so much local countryside that he led resistance and saved the Lye for public recreation. How far-sighted he was, in the days when there must have seemed a never-ending supply of countryside and when people still had little time to enjoy it; The National Trust wasn't even founded until 1895.

The towpath offers many miles of country walking but with five locks here in St Johns there's plenty of activity to watch without walking at all. It's safer than ever too, as modern restoration work has incorporated design changes to reach modern safety standards. Otherwise every effort has been made to re-create the canal as of old, even down to the new bricks being made to the old imperial measurements and set in special 'old-fashioned' mortar, while the curve of the bridges was achieved with the traditional 'hundred foot line' method. Surrey has interest in the most unlikely places and St Johns is just such a place.